THE EDUCATED IMAGINATION

THE EDUCATED IMAGINATION

by Northrop Frye

The Massey Lectures — Second series

CBC Enterprises/les Entreprises Radio-Canada

MONTRÉAL • TORONTO • NEW YORK • LONDON

The Massey Lectures were created in honour of the Right Honourable Vincent Massey, former Governor-General of Canada, and were inaugurated by the CBC in 1961 to enable distinguished authorities to communicate the results of original study or research on a variety of subjects of general interest.

Canadian Cataloguing in Publication Data

Frye, Northrop, 1912-
    The educated imagination

(The Massey lectures; 2nd ser.)
First published: Toronto: Canadian Broadcasting
Corporation, 1963.
Text of 6 radio lectures broadcast in fall, 1962.
ISBN 0-88794-039-0

1. Literature — Addresses, essays, lectures.
2. Literature — Study and teaching — Addresses,
essays, lectures. I. CBC Enterprises. II. Title.
III. Series.

PN45.F72 1983   801   C83-099329-0

Distributed by Stoddart Publishing Co. Limited
34 Lesmill Road
Toronto, Canada
M3B 2T6

Printed and bound in Canada

Acknowledgements

The author has illustrated his text by quoting from the works of various poets. Where necessary, because of copyright, the publishers have obtained the requisite permission to reproduce excerpts from those works, for which acknowledgement is made as follows:

PAGE 10—*The Motive for Metaphor*. Reprinted from 'The Collected Poems of Wallace Stevens', by permission of Alfred A. Knopf, Inc. Copyright 1954 by Wallace Stevens.

PAGE 19—*There is one story and one story only* . . . (To Juan at Winter Solstice), by Robert Graves. International Authors N.Y. From 'Collected Poems 1959'. Cassell & Co. Ltd.

PAGE 21—*If only I am keen and hard like the sheer tip of a wedge* . . . , from 'The Complete Poems of D. H. Lawrence'. Messrs. William Heinemann Ltd., Laurence Pollinger Ltd., and the estate of the late Mrs. Frieda Lawrence.

PAGES 21, 27—*An aged man is but a paltry thing* . . . (Sailing to Byzantium) and *A girl arose that had red mournful lips* . . . (The Sorrow of Love) from 'Collected Poems by W. B. Yeats'. Macmillan Company.

PAGE 27—*I also had my hour* . . . , by G. K. Chesterton. From 'The Wild Knight and Other Poems'. Permission authorized by Miss D. E. Collins and Messrs. J. M. Dent & Sons.

The six radio talks published here are from the second in the yearly series of Massey Lectures, begun by the CBC in 1961 to enable distinguished authorities in fields of general interest and importance to present the results of original study or research. The series was named in honour of the Rt. Hon. Vincent Massey, then Governor-General of Canada, and lectures in it are arranged by the CBC Department of Public Affairs.

HERMAN NORTHROP FRYE was born in Sherbrooke, Quebec in 1912. In 1929 he entered the University of Toronto and, after graduating in 1933 in the Honour Course in Philosophy and English, completed the theological course in Emmanuel College. He was ordained in the United Church of Canada in 1936.

Realizing that his vocation lay in university teaching, he went to Merton College, Oxford, and received the Oxford M.A. in 1940, after being graduated with first class honours in the English School. He joined the Department of English in Victoria College as a Lecturer in 1939, and became Assistant Professor in 1942, Associate Professor in 1946, Professor in 1947, Chairman of the Department of English (Victoria College) in 1952, and Principal of Victoria College in 1959. On January 1, 1967, he retired from the Principalship and became University Professor in the University of Toronto, remaining also a Professor of English at Victoria. He was named Chancellor of Victoria Univeristy in 1978.

He has been a Fellow of the Royal Society of Canada since 1951. In 1958 he received the Royal Society's Lorne Pierce Medal, in 1967 the Canada Council Medal, the Royal Society's Pierre Chauveau Medal in 1970 and the Canada Council Molson Prize in 1971, for distinguished contributions to Canadian literature. He received the Royal Bank Award in 1978. He was elected a Foreign Honorary Member of the American Academy of Arts and Sciences in 1969 and was made a Companion of the Order of Canada in 1972. In 1974 he was made an honorary Fellow of Merton College, Oxford, and received a Civic Honour from the City of Toronto. He was made a Corresponding Fellow of the British Academy in 1975, and a Foreign Member of the American Academy and Institute of Arts and Letters in 1981.

Professor Frye has lectured at over a hundred universities in the United States, Canada, Great Britain, Ireland, Scandinavia, Japan, New Zealand, Italy and Israel, and has taught a full term or a summer session in Harvard, Columbia, Princeton, Indiana, Washington, British Columbia, Cornell, Berkeley and Oxford. He has given many special lectures on endowed lecture foundations.

His chief publications are: *Fearful Symmetry: A Study of William Blake*, 1947; *Anatomy of Criticism*, 1957; *The Well-Tempered Critic*, 1963; *The Educated Imagination*, 1963; *T. S. Eliot*, 1963; *Fables of Identity*, 1963; *A Natural Perspective*, 1965; *The Return of Eden*, 1965; *Fools of Time*, 1967; *The Modern Century*, 1967; *A Study of English Romanticism*, 1968; *The Stubborn Structure*, 1970; *The Bush Garden*, 1971; *The Critical Path*, 1971; *The Secular Scripture*, 1976; *Spiritus Mundi*, 1976; *Northrop Frye on Culture and Literature*, 1978; *Creation and Recreation*, 1980; *The Great Code*, 1982; *Divisions on Ground*, 1982; *The Myth of Deliverance: Reflections on Shakespeare's Problem Comedies*, 1983.

CONTENTS

THE MOTIVE FOR METAPHOR 1

For the past twenty-five years I have been teaching and studying English literature in a university. As in any other job, certain questions stick in one's mind, not because people keep asking them, but because they're the questions inspired by the very fact of being in such a place. What good is the study of literature? Does it help us to think more clearly, or feel more sensitively, or live a better life than we could without it? What is the function of the teacher and scholar, or of the person who calls himself, as I do, a literary critic? What difference does the study of literature make in our social or political or religious attitude? In my early days I thought very little about such questions, not because I had any of the answers, but because I assumed that anybody who asked them was naïve. I think now that the simplest questions are not only the hardest to answer, but the most important to ask, so I'm going to raise them and try to suggest what my present answers are. I say try to suggest, because there are only more or less inadequate answers to such questions—there aren't any right answers. The kind of problem that literature raises is not the kind that you ever 'solve'. Whether my answers are any good or not, they represent a fair amount of thinking about the questions. As I can't see my audience, I have to choose my rhetorical style in the dark, and I'm taking the classroom style, because an audience of students is the one I feel easiest with.

There are two things in particular that I want to discuss with you. In school, and in university, there's a subject called 'English' in English-speaking countries. English means, in the first place, the mother tongue. As that, it's the most practical subject in the world: you can't understand anything or take any part in your society without it. Wherever illiteracy is a problem, it's as fundamental a problem as getting enough to eat or a place to sleep. The native language takes precedence over every other subject of study: nothing else can compare with it in usefulness. But then you find that every mother tongue, in any developed or civilized society, turns into something called literature. If you keep on studying 'English', you find yourself trying to read Shakespeare and Milton. Literature, we're told, is one of the arts, along with painting and music, and, after you've looked up all the hard words and the Classical allusions and learned what words like imagery and diction are supposed to mean, what you use in understanding it, or so you're told, is your imagination. Here you don't seem to be in quite the same practical and useful area: Shakespeare and Milton, whatever their merits, are not the kind of thing you must know to hold any place in society at all. A person who knows nothing about literature may be an ignoramus, but many people don't mind being that. Every child realizes that literature is taking him in a different direction from the immediately useful, and a good many children complain loudly about this. Two questions I want to deal with, then, are, first: what is the relation of English as the mother tongue to English as a literature? Second: what is the social value of the study of literature, and what is the place of the imagination that literature addresses itself to, in the learning process?

Let's start with the different ways there are of dealing with the world we're living in. Suppose you're shipwrecked on an uninhabited island in the South Seas. The first thing you do is to take a long look at the world around you, a world of sky and sea and earth and stars and trees and hills. You see this world as objective, as something set over against you and not yourself or related to you in any way. And you notice two things about this objective world. In the first place, it doesn't have any conversation. It's full of animals and plants and insects going on with their own business, but there's nothing that responds to you: it has no morals and no intelligence, or at least none that you can grasp. It may have a shape and a meaning, but it doesn't seem to be a human shape or a human meaning. Even if there's enough to eat and no dangerous animals, you feel lonely and frightened and unwanted in such a world.

In the second place, you find that looking at the world, as something set over against you, splits your mind in two. You have an intellect that feels curious about it and wants to study it, and you have feelings or emotions that see it as beautiful or austere or terrible. You know that both these attitudes have some reality, at least for you. If the ship you were wrecked in was a Western ship, you'd probably feel that your intellect tells you more about what's really there in the outer world, and that your emotions tell you more about what's going on inside you. If your background were Oriental, you'd be more likely to reverse this and say that the beauty or terror was what was really there, and that your instinct to count and classify and measure and pull to pieces was what was inside your mind. But whether your point of view is Western or Eastern, intellect and emotion never get together in your mind as long as you're simply looking at the world. They alternate, and keep you divided between them.

The language you use on this level of the mind is the language of consciousness or awareness. It's largely a language of nouns and adjectives. You have to have names for things, and you need qualities like 'wet' or 'green' or 'beautiful' to describe how things seem to you. This is the speculative or contemplative position of the mind, the position in which the arts and sciences begin, although they don't stay there very long. The sciences begin by accepting the facts and the evidence about an outside world without trying to alter them. Science proceeds by accurate measurement and description, and follows the demands of the reason rather than the emotions. What it deals with is there, whether we like it or not. The emotions are unreasonable: for them it's what they like and don't like that comes first. We'd be naturally inclined to think that the arts follow the path of emotion, in contrast to the sciences. Up to a point they do, but there's a complicating factor.

That complicating factor is the contrast between 'I like this' and 'I don't like this'. In this Robinson Crusoe life I've assigned you, you may have moods of complete peacefulness and joy, moods when you accept your island and everything around you. You wouldn't have such moods very often, and when you had them, they'd be moods of identification, when you felt that the island was a part of you and you a part of it. That is not the feeling of consciousness or awareness, where you feel split off from everything that's not your perceiving self. Your habitual state of mind is the feeling of separation which goes with being conscious, and the feeling 'this is not a part of me' soon becomes 'this is not what I want'. Notice the word 'want': we'll be coming back to it.

So you soon realize that there's a difference between the world you're living in and the world you want to live in. The world you want to live in is a human world, not an objective one: it's not an environment but a home; it's not the world you see but the world you build out of what you see. You go to work to build a shelter or plant a garden, and as soon as you start to work you've moved into a different level of human life. You're not separating only yourself from nature now, but constructing a human world and separating it from the rest of the world. Your intellect and emotions are now both engaged in the same activity, so there's no longer any real distinction between them. As soon as you plant a garden or a crop, you develop the conception of a 'weed', the plant you don't want in there. But you can't say that 'weed' is either an intellectual or an emotional conception, because it's both at once. Further, you go to work because you feel you have to, and because you want something at the end of the work. That means that the important categories of your life are no longer the subject and the object, the watcher and the things being watched: the important categories are what you have to do and what you want to do—in other words, necessity and freedom.

One person by himself is not a complete human being, so I'll provide you with another shipwrecked refugee of the opposite sex and an eventual family. Now you're a member of a human society. This human society after a while will transform the island into something with a human shape. What that human shape is, is revealed in the shape of the work you do: the buildings, such as they are, the paths through the woods, the planted crops fenced off against whatever animals want to eat them. These things, these rudiments of city, highway, garden and farm, are the human form of nature, or the form of human nature, whichever you like. This is the area of the applied arts and sciences, and it appears in our society as engineering and agriculture and medicine and architecture. In this area we can never say clearly where the art stops and the science begins, or vice versa.

The language you use on this level is the language of practical sense, a language of verbs or words of action and movement. The practical world, however, is a world where actions speak louder than words. In some ways it's a higher level of existence than the speculative level, because it's doing something about the world instead of just looking at it, but in itself it's a much more primitive level. It's the process of adapting to the environment, or rather of transforming the environment in the interests of one species, that goes on among animals and plants as well as human beings. The animals have a good many of our practical skills: some insects make pretty fair architects, and beavers know quite a lot about engineering. In this island, probably, and certainly if you were alone, you'd have about the ranking of a second-rate animal. What makes our practical life really human is a third level of the mind, a level where consciousness and practical skill come together.

This third level is a vision or model in your mind of what you want to construct. There's that word 'want' again. The actions of man are prompted by desire, and some of these desires are needs, like food and warmth and shelter. One of these needs is sexual, the desire to reproduce and bring more human beings into existence. But there's also a desire to bring a social human form into existence: the form of cities and gardens and farms that we call civilization. Many animals and insects have this social form too, but man knows that he has it: he can compare what he does with what he can imagine being done. So we begin to see where the imagination belongs in the scheme of human affairs. It's the power of constructing possible models of human experience. In the world of the imagination, anything goes that's imaginatively possible, but nothing really happens. If it did happen, it would move out of the world of imagination into the world of action.

We have three levels of the mind now, and a language for each of them, which in English-speaking societies means an English for each of them. There's the level of consciousness and awareness, where the most important thing is the difference between me and everything else. The English of this level is the English of ordinary conversation, which is mostly monologue, as you'll soon realize if you do a bit of eavesdropping, or listening to yourself. We can call it the language of self-expression. Then there's the level of social participation, the working or technological language of teachers and preachers and politicians and advertisers and lawyers and journalists and scientists. We've already called this the language of practical sense. Then there's the level of imagination, which produces the literary language of poems and plays and novels. They're not really different languages, of course, but three different reasons for using words.

On this basis, perhaps, we can distinguish the arts from the sciences. Science begins with the world we have to live in, accepting its data and trying to explain its laws. From there, it moves towards the imagination: it becomes a mental construct, a model of a possible way of interpreting experience. The further it goes in this direction, the more it tends to speak the language of mathematics, which is really one of the languages of the imagination, along with literature and music. Art, on the other hand, begins with the world we construct, not with the world we see. It starts with the imagination, and then works towards ordinary experience: that is, it tries to make itself as convincing and recognizable as it can. You can see why we tend to think of the sciences as intellectual and the arts as emotional: one starts with the world as it is, the other with the world we want to have. Up to a point it is true that science gives an intellectual view of reality, and that the arts try to make the emotions as precise and disciplined as sciences do the intellect. But of course it's nonsense to think of the scientist as a cold unemotional reasoner and the artist as somebody who's in a perpetual emotional tizzy. You can't distinguish the arts from the sciences by the mental processes the people in them use: they both operate on a mixture of hunch and common sense. A highly developed science and a highly developed art are very close together, psychologically and other-wise.

Still, the fact that they start from opposite ends, even if they do meet in the middle, makes for one important difference between them. Science learns more and more about the world as it goes on: it evolves and improves. A physicist today knows more physics than Newton did, even if he's not as great a scientist. But literature begins with the possible model of experience, and what it produces is the literary model we call the classic. Literature doesn't evolve or improve or progress. We may have dramatists in the future who will write plays as good as *King Lear*, though they'll be very different ones, but drama as a whole will never get better than *King Lear*. *King Lear* is it, as far as drama is concerned; so is *Oedipus Rex*, written two thousand years earlier than that, and both will be models of dramatic writing as long as the human race endures. Social conditions may improve: most of us would rather live in nineteenth-century United States than in thirteenth-century Italy, and for most of us Whitman's celebration of democracy makes a lot more sense than Dante's Inferno. But it doesn't follow that Whitman is a better poet than Dante: literature won't line up with that kind of improvement.

So we find that everything that does improve, including science, leaves the literary artist out in the cold. Writers don't seem to benefit much by the advance of science, although they thrive on superstitions of all kinds. And you certainly wouldn't turn to contemporary poets for guidance or leadership in the twentieth-century world. You'd hardly go to Ezra Pound, with his fascism and social credit and Confucianism and anti-semitism. Or to Yeats, with his spiritualism and fairies and astrology. Or to D. H. Lawrence, who'll tell you that it's a good thing for servants to be flogged because that restores the precious current of blood-reciprocity between servant and master. Or to T. S. Eliot, who'll tell you that to have a flourishing culture we should educate an élite, keep most people living in the same spot, and never disestablish the Church of England. The novelists seem to be a little closer to the world they're living in, but not much. When Communists talk about the decadence of bourgeois culture, this is the kind of thing they always bring up. Their own writers don't seem to be any better, though; just duller. So the real question is a bigger one. Is it possible that literature, especially poetry, is something that a scientific civilization like ours will eventually outgrow? Man has always wanted to fly, and thousands of years ago he was making sculptures of winged bulls and telling stories about people who flew so high on artificial wings that the sun melted them off. In an Indian play fifteen hundred years old, *Sakuntala,* there's a god who flies around in a chariot that to a modern reader sounds very much like a private aeroplane. Interesting that the writer had so much imagination, but do we need such stories now that we have private aeroplanes?

This is not a new question: it was raised a hundred and fifty years ago by Thomas Love Peacock, who was a poet and novelist himself, and a very brilliant one. He wrote an essay called *Four Ages of Poetry,* with his tongue of course in his cheek, in which he said that poetry was the mental rattle that awakened the imagination of mankind in its infancy, but that now, in an age of science and technology, the poet has outlived his social function. 'A poet in our times,' said Peacock, 'is a semi-barbarian in a civilized community. He lives in the days that are past. His ideas, thoughts, feelings, associations, are all with barbarous manners, obsolete customs, and exploded superstitions. The march of his intellect is like that of a crab, backwards.' Peacock's essay annoyed his friend Shelley, who wrote another essay called *A Defence of Poetry* to refute it. Shelley's essay is a wonderful piece of writing, but it's not likely to convince anyone who needs convincing. I shall be spending a good deal of my time on this question of the relevance of literature in the world of today, and I can only indicate the general lines my answer will take. There are two points I can make now, one simple, the other more difficult.

The simple point is that literature belongs to the world man constructs, not to the world he sees; to his home, not his environment. Literature's world is a concrete human world of immediate experience. The poet uses images and objects and sensations much more than he uses abstract ideas; the novelist is concerned with telling stories, not with working out arguments. The world of literature is human in shape, a world where the sun rises in the east and sets in the west over the edge of a flat earth in three dimensions, where the primary realities are not atoms or electrons but bodies, and the primary forces not energy or gravitation but love and death and passion and joy. It's not surprising if writers are often rather simple people, not always what we think of as intellectuals, and certainly not always any freer of silliness or perversity than anyone else. What concerns us is what they produce, not what they are, and poetry, according to Milton, who ought to have known, is 'more simple, sensuous and passionate' than philosophy or science.

The more difficult point takes us back to what we said when we were on that South Sea island. Our emotional reaction to the world varies from 'I like this' to 'I don't like this'. The first, we said, was a state of identity, a feeling that everything around us was part of us, and the second is the ordinary state of consciousness, or separation, where art and science begin. Art begins as soon as 'I don't like this' turns into 'this is not the way I could imagine it'. We notice in passing that the creative and the neurotic minds have a lot in common. They're both dissatisfied with what they see; they both believe that something else ought to be there, and they try to pretend it is there or to make it be there. The differences are more important, but we're not ready for them yet.

At the level of ordinary consciousness the individual man is the centre of everything, surrounded on all sides by what he isn't. At the level of practical sense, or civilization, there's a human circumference, a little cultivated world with a human shape, fenced off from the jungle and inside the sea and the sky. But in the imagination anything goes that can be imagined, and the limit of the imagination is a totally human world. Here we recapture, in full consciousness, that original lost sense of identity with our surroundings, where there is nothing outside the mind of man, or something identical with the mind of man. Religions present us with visions of eternal and infinite heavens or paradises which have the form of the cities and gardens of human civilization, like the Jerusalem and Eden of the Bible, completely separated from the state of frustration and misery that bulks so large in ordinary life. We're not concerned with these visions as religion, but they indicate what the limits of the imagination are. They indicate too that in the human world the imagination has no limits, if you follow me. We said that the desire to fly produced the aeroplane. But people don't get into planes because they want to fly; they get into planes because they want to get somewhere else faster. What's produced the aeroplane is not so much a desire to fly as a rebellion against the tyranny of time and space. And that's a process that can never stop, no matter how high our Titovs and Glenns may go.

For each of these six talks I've taken a title from some work of literature, and my title for this one is 'The Motive for Metaphor', from a poem of Wallace Stevens. Here's the poem:

> You like it under the trees in autumn,
> Because everything is half dead.
> The wind moves like a cripple among the leaves
> And repeats words without meaning.
>
> In the same way, you were happy in spring,
> With the half colors of quarter-things,
> The slightly brighter sky, the melting clouds,
> The single bird, the obscure moon—
>
> The obscure moon lighting an obscure world
> Of things that would never be quite expressed,
> Where you yourself were never quite yourself
> And did not want nor have to be,
>
> Desiring the exhilarations of changes:
> The motive for metaphor, shrinking from
> The weight of primary noon,
> The A B C of being,
>
> The ruddy temper, the hammer
> Of red and blue, the hard sound—
> Steel against intimation—the sharp flash,
> The vital, arrogant, fatal, dominant X.

What Stevens calls the weight of primary noon, the A B C of being, and the dominant X is the objective world, the world set over against us. Outside literature, the main motive for writing is to describe this world. But literature itself uses language in a way which associates our minds with it. As soon as you use associative language, you begin using figures of speech. If you say this talk is dry and dull, you're using figures associating it with bread and breadknives. There are two main kinds of association, analogy and identity, two things that are like each other and two things that are each other. You can say with Burns, 'My love's like a red, red rose', or you can say with Shakespeare:

Thou that art now the world's fresh ornament
And only herald to the gaudy spring.

One produces the figure of speech called the simile; the other produces the figure called metaphor.

In descriptive writing you have to be careful of associative language. You'll find that analogy, or likeness to something else, is very tricky to handle in description, because the differences are as important as the resemblances. As for metaphor, where you're really saying 'this *is* that', you're turning your back on logic and reason completely, because logically two things can never be the same thing and still remain two things. The poet, however, uses these two crude, primitive, archaic forms of thought in the most uninhibited way, because his job is not to describe nature, but to show you a world completely absorbed and possessed by the human mind. So he produces what Baudelaire called a 'suggestive magic including at the same time object and subject, the world outside the artist and the artist himself'. The motive for metaphor, according to Wallace Stevens, is a desire to associate, and finally to identify, the human mind with what goes on outside it, because the only genuine joy you can have is in those rare moments when you feel that although we may know in part, as Paul says, we are also a part of what we know.

THE SINGING SCHOOL   2

In my first talk I shipwrecked you on a South Sea island and tried to distinguish the attitudes of mind that might result. I suggested that there would be three main attitudes. First, a state of consciousness or awareness that separates you as an individual from the rest of the world. Second, a practical attitude of creating a human way of life in that world. Third, an imaginative attitude, a vision or model of the world as you could imagine it and would like it to be. I said that there was a language for each attitude, and that these languages appear in our society as the language of ordinary conversation, the language of practical skills, and the language of literature. We discovered that the language of literature was associative: it uses figures of speech, like the simile and the metaphor, to suggest an identity between the human mind and the world outside it, that identity being what the imagination is chiefly concerned with.

You notice that we've gradually shifted off the island back to twentieth-century Canada. There'd be precious little literature produced on your island, and what there'd be would be of a severely practical kind, like messages in bottles, if you had any bottles. The reason for that is that you're not a genuine primitive:

your imagination couldn't operate on such a world except in terms of the world you know. We'll see how important a point this is in a moment. In the meantime, think of Robinson Crusoe, an eighteenth-century Englishman from a nation of shop-keepers. He didn't write poetry: what he did was to open a journal and a ledger.

But suppose you were enough of a primitive to develop a genuinely imaginative life of your own. You'd start by identifying the human and the non-human worlds in all sorts of ways. The commonest, and the most important for literature, is the god, the being who is human in general form and character, but seems to have some particular connexion with the outer world, a storm-god or sun-god or tree-god. Some peoples identify themselves with certain animals or plants, called totems; some link certain animals, real or imaginary, bulls or dragons, with forces of nature; some ascribe powers of controlling nature to certain human beings, usually magicians, sometimes kings. You may say that these things belong to comparative religion or anthropology, not to literary criticism. I'm saying that they are all products of an impulse to identify human and natural worlds; that they're really metaphors, and become purely metaphors, part of the language of poetry, as soon as they cease to be beliefs, or even sooner. Horace, in a particularly boastful mood, once said his verse would last as long as the vestal virgins kept going up the Capitoline Hill to worship at the temple of Jupiter. But Horace's poetry has lasted longer than Jupiter's religion, and Jupiter himself has only survived because he disappeared into literature.

No human society is too primitive to have some kind of literature. The only thing is that primitive literature hasn't yet become distinguished from other aspects of life: it's still embedded in religion, magic, and social ceremonies. But we can see literary expression taking shape in these things, and forming an imaginative framework, so to speak, that contains the literature descending from it. Stories are told about gods, and form a mythology. The gods take on certain characteristics: there's a trickster god, a mocking god, a boastful god: the same types of characters get into legends and folk tales and, as literature develops, into fiction. Rituals and dances take on dramatic form, and eventually an independent drama develops. Poems used for certain occasions, war-songs, work-songs, funeral laments, lullabies, become traditional literary forms.

The moral of all this is that every form in literature has a pedigree, and we can trace its descent back to the earliest times. A writer's desire to write can only have come from previous experience of literature, and he'll start by imitating whatever he's read, which usually means what the people around him are writing. This provides for him what is called a convention, a certain typical and socially accepted way of writing. The young poet of Shakespeare's day would probably write about the frustration of sexual desire; a young poet today would probably write about the release of it, but in both cases the writing is conventional. After working in this convention for a while, his own distinctive sense of form will develop out of his knowledge of literary technique. He doesn't create out of nothing; and whatever he has to say he can only say in a recognizably literary way. We can perhaps understand this better if we take painting as our example. There have been painters since the last ice age, and I hope there'll be painters until the next one: they show every conceivable variety of vision, and of originality in setting it out. But the actual technical or formal problems of composition involved in the act of getting certain colours and shapes on a flat surface, usually rectangular, have remained constant from the beginning.

So with literature. In fiction, the technical problems of shaping a story to make it interesting to read, to provide for suspense, to find the logical points where the story should begin and end, don't change much in whatever time or culture the story's being told. E. M. Forster once remarked that if it weren't for wedding bells or funeral bells a novelist would hardly know where to stop: he might have added a third conventional ending, the point of self-knowledge, at which a character finds something out about himself as a result of some crucial experience. But weddings and deaths and initiation ceremonies have always been points at which the creative imagination came into focus, both now and thousands of years ago. If you open the Bible, you'll soon come to the story of the finding of the infant Moses by Pharaoh's daughter. That's a conventional type of story, the mysterious birth of the hero. It was told about a Mesopotamian king long before there was any Bible; it was told of Perseus in Greek legend; then it passed into literature with Euripides' play *Ion*; then it was used by Plautus and Terence and other writers of comedies; then it became a device in fiction, used in *Tom Jones* and *Oliver Twist*, and it's still going strong.

You notice that popular literature, the kind of stories that are read for relaxation, is always very highly conventionalized. If you pick up a detective story, you may not know until the last page who done it, but you always know before you start reading exactly the kind of thing that's going to happen. If you read the fiction in women's magazines, you read the story of Cinderella over and over again. If you read thrillers, you read the story of Bluebeard over and over again. If you read Westerns, you're reading a development of a pastoral convention, which turns up in writers of all ages, including Shakespeare. It's the same with characterization. The tricky or boastful gods of ancient myths and primitive folk tales are characters of the same kind that turn up in Faulkner or Tennessee Williams. I mentioned Plautus and Terence, writers of comedies in Rome two hundred years before Christ, who took their plots mainly from still earlier Greek plays. Usually what happens is that a young man is in love with a courtesan; his father says nothing doing, but a clever slave fools the father and the young man gets his girl. Change the courtesan to a chorus-girl, the slave to a butler and the father to Aunt Agatha, and you've got the same plot and the same cast of characters that you find in a novel of P. G. Wodehouse. Wodehouse is a popular writer, and the fact that he is a popular writer has a lot to do with his use of stock plots. Of course he doesn't take his own plots seriously; he makes fun of them by the way he uses them; but so did Plautus and Terence.

Our principle is, then, that literature can only derive its forms from itself: they can't exist outside literature, any more than musical forms like the sonata and the fugue can exist outside music. This principle is important for understanding what's happened in Canadian literature. When Canada was still a country for pioneers, it was assumed that a new country, a new society, new things to look at and new experiences would produce a new literature. So Canadian writers ever since, including me, have been saying that Canada was just about to get itself a brand new literature. But these new things provide only content; they don't provide new literary forms. Those can come only from the literature Canadians already know. People coming to Canada from, say, England in 1830 started writing in the conventions of English literature in 1830. They couldn't possibly have done anything else: they weren't primitives, and could never have looked at the world the way the Indians did. When they wrote, they produced second-hand imitations of Byron and Scott and Tom Moore, because that was what they had been reading; Canadian writers today produce imitations of D. H. Lawrence and W. H. Auden for the same reason.

The same thing happened in the States, and people predicted that new Iliads and Odysseys would arise in the ancient forests of the new world. The Americans were a little luckier than we were: they really did have writers original enough to give them their national epics. These national epics weren't a bit like the Iliad or the Odyssey; they were such books as *Huckleberry Finn* and *Moby Dick*, which developed out of conventions quite different from Homer's. Or is it really true to say that they're not a bit like the Iliad or the Odyssey? Superficially they're very different, but the better you know both the Odyssey and *Huckleberry Finn*, the more impressed you'll be by the resemblances: the disguises, the ingenious lies to get out of scrapes, the exciting adventures that often suddenly turn tragic, the mingling of the strange and the familiar, the sense of a human comradeship stronger than any disaster. And Melville goes out of his way to explain how his white whale belongs in the same family of sea monsters that turn up in Greek myths and in the Bible.

I'm not saying that there's nothing new in literature: I'm saying that everything is new, and yet recognizably the same kind of thing as the old, just as a new baby is a genuinely new individual, although it's also an example of something very common, which is human beings, and also it's lineally descended from the first human beings there ever were. And what, you ask, is the point of saying that? I have two points.

First: you remember that I distinguished the language of imagination, or literature, from the language of consciousness, which produces ordinary conversation, and from the language of practical skill or knowledge, which produces information, like science and history. These are both forms of verbal address, where you speak directly to an audience. There is no direct address in literature: it isn't what you say but how it's said that's important there. The literary writer isn't giving information, either about a subject or about his state of mind: he's trying to let something take on its own form, whether it's a poem or play or novel or whatever. That's why you can't produce literature voluntarily, in the way you'd write a letter or a report. That's also why it's no use telling the poet that he ought to write in a different way so you can understand him better. The writer of literature can only write out what takes shape in his mind. It's quite wrong to think of the original writer as the opposite of the conventional one. All writers are conventional, because all writers have the same problem of transferring their language from direct speech to the imagination. For the serious mediocre writer convention makes him sound like a lot of other people; for the popular writer it gives him a formula he can exploit; for the serious good writer it releases his experiences or emotions from himself and incorporates them into literature, where they belong.

Here's a poem by a contemporary of Shakespeare, Thomas Campion:

When thou must home to shades of underground,
And there arriv'd, a new admired guest,
The beauteous spirits do engirt thee round,
White Iope, blithe Helen, and the rest,
To hear the stories of thy finish'd love
From that smooth tongue whose music hell can move;

Then wilt thou speak of banqueting delights,
Of masques and revels which sweet youth did make,
Of tourneys and great challenges of knights,
And all these triumphs for thy beauty's sake:
When thou hast told these honours done to thee,
Then tell, O tell, how thou didst murder me.

This is written in the convention that poets of that age used for love poetry: the poet is always in love with some obdurate and unresponsive mistress, whose neglect of the lover may even cause his madness or death. It's pure convention, and it's a complete waste of time trying to find out about the women in Campion's life—there can't possibly be any real experience behind it. Campion himself was a poet and critic, and a composer who set his poems to his own musical settings. He was also a professional man who started out in law but switched over to medicine, and served for some time in the army. In other words, he was a busy man, who didn't have much time for getting himself murdered by cruel mistresses. The poem uses religious language, but not a religion that Campion could ever have believed in. At the same time it's a superbly lovely poem; it's perfection itself, and if you think that a conventional poem can only be just a literary exercise, and that you could write a better poem out of real experience, I'd be doubtful of your success. But I can't explain what Campion has really done in this poem without my second point.

All themes and characters and stories that you encounter in literature belong to one big interlocking family. You can see how true this is if you think of such words as tragedy or comedy or satire or romance: certain typical ways in which stories get told. You keep associating your literary experiences together: you're always being reminded of some other story you read or movie you saw or character that impressed you. For most of us, most of the time, this goes on unconsciously, but the fact that it does go on suggests that perhaps in literature you don't just read one novel or poem after another, but that there's a real subject to be studied, as there is in a science, and that the more you read, the more you learn about literature as a whole. This conception of 'literature as a whole' suggests something else. Is it possible to get, in however crude and sketchy a way, some bird's eye view of what literature as a whole is about: considered, that is, as a coherent subject of study and not just a pile of books? Several critics in the last few years have been playing with this suggestion, and they all begin by going back to the primitive literature that we spoke of a moment ago.

For constructing any work of art you need some principle of repetition or recurrence: that's what gives you rhythm in music and pattern in painting. A literature, we said, has a lot to do with identifying the human world with the natural world around it, or finding analogies between them. In nature the most obvious repeating or recurring feature is the cycle. The sun travels across the sky into the dark and comes back again; the seasons go from spring to winter and back to spring again; water goes from springs or fountains to the sea and back again in rain. Human life goes from childhood to death and back again in a new birth. A great many primitive stories and myths, then, would attach themselves to this cycle which stretches like a backbone through the middle of both human and natural life.

Mythologies are full of young gods or heroes who go through various successful adventures and then are deserted or betrayed and killed, and then come back to life again, suggesting in their story the movement of the sun across the sky into the dark or the progression of seasons through winter and spring. Sometimes they're swallowed by a huge sea monster or killed by a boar; or they wander in a strange dark underworld and then fight their way out again. Myths of this kind come into the stories of Perseus, Theseus and Hercules in Greek myth, and they lurk behind many of the stories of the Bible. Usually there's a female figure in the story. Some of the critics I mentioned suggest that these stories go back to a single mythical story, which may never have existed as a whole story anywhere, but which we can reconstruct from the myths and legends we have. The poet Robert Graves has tried to do this, in a book called *The White Goddess*. Graves has a poem called *To Juan at the Winter Solstice*: Juan is his son, and the winter solstice is Christmas time, the low point of the year, when we set logs on fire or hang lights on a tree, originally to help make sure that the light of the world won't go out altogether. Graves's poem begins:

There is one story and one story only
That will prove worth your telling,
Whether as learned bard or gifted child;
To it all lines or lesser gauds belong
That startle with their shining
Such common stories as they stray into.

In Graves's version of the one story, the heroine is a 'white goddess', a female figure associated with the moon, who is sometimes a maiden, sometimes a wife, sometimes a beautiful but treacherous witch or siren, sometimes a sinister old woman or hag belonging to the lower world, like Hecate and the witches in *Macbeth*. Graves would say that the eloquence and power of the Campion poem I just read you was the result of the fact that it evokes this white goddess in one of her most frequent aspects: the sinister witch in hell gloating over the murdered bodies of her lovers. By saying it's the only story worth telling in literature, Graves means that the great types of stories, such as comedies and tragedies, start out as episodes from it. Comedies derive from the phase in which god and goddess are happy wedded lovers; tragedies from the phase in which the lover is cast off and killed while the white goddess renews her youth and waits for another round of victims.

I think myself that Graves's story is a central one in literature, but that it fits inside a still bigger and better known one. To explain what it is I have to take you back, for the last time, I hope, to the desert island and the three levels of the mind.

You start, I said, by looking at the world with your intellect and your emotions. Occasionally you have a feeling of identity with your surroundings—'I like this'—but more often you feel self-conscious and cut off from them. I mentioned Robinson Crusoe opening his journal and ledger: all he had to put into his ledger were the things against and in favour of his situation, and perhaps now we can see why he thought it was important to record them. If you were developing an imagination in your new world that belonged to that world, you'd start off something like this: I feel separated and cut off from the world around me, but occasionally I've felt that it was really a part of me, and I hope I'll have that feeling again, and that next time it won't go away. That's a dim, misty outline of the story that's told so often, of how man once lived in a golden age or a garden of Eden or the Hesperides, or a happy island kingdom in the Atlantic, how that world was lost, and how we some day may be able to get it back again. I said earlier that this is a feeling of lost identity, and that poetry, by using the language of identification, which is metaphor, tries to lead our imaginations back to it. Anyway, that's what a lot of poets say they're trying to do. Here's Blake:

> The nature of my work is visionary or imaginative; it is an attempt to restore what the ancients called the Golden Age.

Here's Wordsworth:

                  Paradise, and groves
Elysian, Fortunate Fields—like those of old
Sought in the Atlantic Main—why should they be
A history only of departed things,
Or a mere fiction of what never was? ...
I, long before the blissful hour arrives,
Would chant, in lonely peace, the spousal verse
Of this great consummation.

Here's D. H. Lawrence:

If only I am keen and hard like the sheer tip of a wedge
Driven by invisible blows,
The rock will split, we shall come at the wonder, we shall find
    the Hesperides.

And here's Yeats, in his poem *Sailing to Byzantium*, which has given me the title I have given to this talk, 'The Singing School':

An aged man is but a paltry thing,
A tattered coat upon a stick, unless
Soul clap its hands and sing, and louder sing
For every tatter in its mortal dress,
Nor is there singing school but studying
Monuments of its own magnificence;
And therefore I have sailed the seas and come
To the holy city of Byzantium.

This story of the loss and regaining of identity is, I think, the framework of all literature. Inside it comes the story of the hero with a thousand faces, as one critic calls him, whose adventures, death, disappearance and marriage or resurrection are the focal points of what later become romance and tragedy and satire and comedy in fiction, and the emotional moods that take their place in such forms as the lyric, which normally doesn't tell a story.

We notice that modern writers speak of these visions of sacred golden cities and happy gardens very rarely, though when they do they clearly mean what they say. They spend a good deal more of their time on the misery, frustration or absurdity of human existence. In other words, literature not only leads us toward the regaining of identity, but it also separates this state from its opposite, the world we don't like and want to get away from. The tone literature takes toward this world is not a moralizing tone, but the tone we call ironic. The effect of irony is to enable us to see over the head of a situation—we have irony in a play, for example, when we know more about what's going on than the characters do—and so to detach us, at least in imagination, from the world we'd prefer not to be involved with.

As civilization develops, we become more preoccupied with human life, and less conscious of our relation to non-human nature. Literature reflects this, and the more advanced the civilization, the more literature seems to concern itself with purely human problems and conflicts. The gods and heroes of the old myths fade away and give place to people like ourselves. In Shakespeare we can still have heroes who can see ghosts and talk in magnificent poetry, but by the time we get to Beckett's *Waiting for Godot* they're speaking prose and have turned into ghosts themselves. We have to look at the figures of speech a writer uses, his images and symbols, to realize that underneath all the complexity of human life that uneasy stare at an alien nature is still haunting us, and the problem of surmounting it still with us. Above all, we have to look at the total design of a writer's work, the title he gives to it, and his main theme, which means his point in writing it, to understand that literature is still doing the same job that mythology did earlier, but filling in its huge cloudy shapes with sharper lights and deeper shadows.

GIANTS IN TIME 3

In the last two talks we've been circling around the question:
what kind of reality does literature have? When you see a play
of Shakespeare, you know that there never were any such people
as Hamlet or Falstaff. There may once have been a prince in
Denmark named Amleth, or there may have been somebody
called Sir John Fastolf—in fact there was, and he comes into an
earlier play of Shakespeare's. But these historical figures have no
more to do with Shakespeare's Hamlet or Falstaff than you or
I have. Poets are fond of telling people, especially people with
money or influence, that they can make them immortal by men-
tioning them in poems. Sometimes they're right. If there ever
was any huge sulky bruiser in the Greek army named Achilles,
he'd no doubt be surprised to find that his name was still well
known after three thousand years. Whether he'd be pleased or
not is another question. Assuming that there was a historical
Achilles, there are two reasons why his name is still well known.
One reason is that Homer wrote about him. The other reason
is that practically everything Homer said about him was prepos-
terous. Nobody was ever made invulnerable by being dipped in

a river; nobody ever fought with a river god; nobody had a sea-nymph for a mother. Whether it's Achilles or Hamlet or King Arthur or Charles Dickens's father, once anyone gets put into literature he's taken over by literature, and whatever he was in real life could hardly matter less. Still, if Homer's Achilles isn't the real Achilles, he isn't unreal either; unrealities don't seem so full of life after three thousand years as Homer's Achilles does. This is the kind of problem we have to tackle next: the fact that what we meet in literature is neither real nor unreal. We have two words, imaginary, meaning unreal, and imaginative, meaning what the writer produces, and they mean entirely different things.

We can understand though how the poet got his reputation as a kind of licensed liar. The word poet itself means liar in some languages, and the words we use in literary criticism, fable, fiction, myth, have all come to mean something we can't believe. Some parents in Victorian times wouldn't let their children read novels because they weren't 'true'. But not many reasonable people to-day would deny that the poet is entitled to change whatever he likes when he uses a theme from history or real life. The reason why was explained long ago by Aristotle. The historian makes specific and particular statements, such as: 'The battle of Hastings was fought in 1066.' Consequently he's judged by the truth or falsehood of what he says—either there was such a battle or there wasn't, and if there was he's got the date either right or wrong. But the poet, Aristotle says, never makes any real statements at all, certainly no particular or specific ones. The poet's job is not to tell you what happened, but what happens: not what did take place, but the kind of thing that always does take place. He gives you the typical, recurring, or what Aristotle calls universal event. You wouldn't go to *Macbeth* to learn about the history of Scotland—you go to it to learn what a man feels like after he's gained a kingdom and lost his soul. When you meet such a character as Micawber in Dickens, you don't feel that there must have been a man Dickens knew who was exactly like this: you feel that there's a bit of Micawber in almost everybody you know, including yourself. Our impressions of human life are picked up one by one, and remain for most of us loose and dis-organized. But we constantly find things in literature that suddenly co-ordinate and bring into focus a great many such impressions, and this is part of what Aristotle means by the typical or universal human event.

All right: but how does this explain Achilles? Achilles was invulnerable except for his heel, and he was the son of a sea-nymph. Neither of these things can be true of anybody, so how does that make Achilles a typical or universal figure? Here there's another kind of principle involved. We said earlier that the more realistic a writer is, and the more his characters and incidents seem to be people like ourselves, the more apt he is to become ironic, which involves putting you, as the reader, in a position of superiority to them, so that you can detach your imagination from the world they live in by seeing it clearly and in the round. Homer's Achilles represents the opposite technique, where the character is a hero, much larger than life. Achilles is more than what any man could be, because he's also what a man wishes he could be, and he does what most men would do if they were strong enough. He's not a portrait of an individual hero, but a great smouldering force of human desire and frustration and discontent, something we all have in us too, part of mankind as a whole. And because he's that he can be partly a god, involved with nature to the point of having a mother in the sea and an enemy in the river, besides having other gods in the sky directly interested in him and what he's doing. And because with all his superhuman strength he's still up against something he can't understand, there's an ironic perspective too. Nobody cares now about the historical Achilles, if there ever was one, but the mythical Achilles reflects a part of our own lives.

Let's leave this for a bit and turn to the question of imagery. What happens when a poet, say, uses an image, an object in nature, like a flock of sheep or a field of flowers? If he does use them, he's clearly going to make a poetic use of them: they're going to become poetic sheep and poetic flowers, absorbed and digested by literature, set out in literary language and inside literary conventions. What you never get in literature are just the sheep that nibble the grass or just the flowers that bloom in the spring. There's always some literary reason for using them, and that means something in human life that they correspond to or represent or resemble. This correspondence of the natural and the human is one of the things that the word 'symbol' means, so we can say that whenever a writer uses an image, or object from the world around him, he's made it a symbol.

There are several ways of doing this. Besides literature, there are all the verbal structures of practical sense, religion, morality, science, and philosophy; and one of the things literature does is to illustrate them, putting their abstract ideas into concrete images and situations. When it does this deliberately, we have what we call allegory, where the writer is saying, more or less: I don't really mean sheep; I mean something political or religious when I say sheep. I think of sheep because I've just heard, on the radio, someone singing an aria from a Bach cantata, which begins: 'Sheep may safely graze where a good shepherd is watching.' This was on a program of religious music, so I suppose somebody must have assumed that the sheep meant Christians and the good shepherd Christ. They easily could have meant that, although by an accident this particular cantata happens to be a secular one, written in honour of the birthday of some German princeling, so the good shepherd is really the prince and the sheep are his taxpayers. But the sheep are allegorical sheep whether the allegory is political or religious, and if they're allegorical they're literary.

There's a great deal of allegory in literature, much more than we usually realize, but straightforward allegory is out of fashion now: most modern writers dislike having their images pinned down in this specific way, and so modern critics think of allegory as a bit simple-minded. The reason is that allegory, where literature is illustrating moral or political or religious truths, means that both the writer and his public have to be pretty firmly convinced of the reality and importance of those truths, and modern writers and publics, on the whole, aren't.

A more common way of indicating that an image is literary is by allusion to something else in literature. Literature tends to be very allusive, and the central things in literature, the Greek and Roman classics, the Bible, Shakespeare and Milton, are echoed over and over again. To take a simple example: many of you will know G. K. Chesterton's poem on the donkey, which describes how ungainly and ridiculous a beast he is, but that he doesn't care because, as the poem concludes:

> I also had my hour,
> One far fierce hour and sweet:
> There was a shout about my ears,
> And palms before my feet.

The reference to Palm Sunday is not incidental to the poem but the whole point of the poem, and we can't read the poem at all until we've placed the reference. In other poems we get references to Classical myths. There's an early poem of Yeats, called 'The Sorrow of Love', where the second stanza went like this:

> And then you came with those red mournful lips,
> And with you came the whole of the world's tears,
> And all the trouble of her labouring ships,
> And all the trouble of her myriad years.

But Yeats was constantly tinkering with his poems, especially the early ones, and in the final edition of his collected poetry we get this instead:

> A girl arose that had red mournful lips
> And seemed the greatness of the world in tears,
> Doomed like Odysseus and the labouring ships
> And proud as Priam murdered with his peers.

The early version is a vague, and the later one a precise, reference to something else in the literary tradition, and Yeats thought that the precise reference was an improvement.

This allusiveness in literature is significant, because it shows what we've been saying all along, that in literature you don't just read one poem or novel after another, but enter into a complete world of which every work of literature forms part. This affects the writer as much as it does the reader. Many people think that the original writer is always directly inspired by life, and that only commonplace or derivative writers get inspired by books. That's nonsense: the only inspiration worth having is an inspiration that clarifies the form of what's being written, and that's more likely to come from something that already has a literary form. We don't often find that a poem depends completely on an allusion, as Chesterton's poem does, but allusiveness runs all through our literary experience. If we don't know the Bible and the central stories of Greek and Roman literature, we can still read books and see plays, but our knowledge of literature can't grow, just as our knowledge of mathematics can't grow if we don't learn the multiplication table. Here we touch on an educational problem, of what should be read when, that we'll have to come back to later.

I said earlier that there's nothing new in literature that isn't the old reshaped. The latest thing in drama is the theatre of the absurd, a completely wacky form of writing where anything goes and there are no rational rules. In one of these plays, Ionesco's *La Chauve Cantatrice* ('The Bald Soprano' in English), a Mr. and Mrs. Martin are talking. They think they must have seen each other before, and discover that they travelled in the same train that morning, that they have the same name and address, sleep in the same bedroom, and both have a two-year-old daughter named Alice. Eventually Mr. Martin decides that he must be talking to his long lost wife Elizabeth. This scene is built on two of the solidest conventions in literature. One is the ironic situation in which two people are intimately related and yet know nothing about each other; the other is the ancient and often very corny device that critics call the 'recognition scene', where the long lost son and heir turns up from Australia in the last act. What makes the Ionesco scene funny is the fact that it's a parody or take-off of these familiar conventions. The allusiveness of literature is part of its symbolic quality, its capacity to absorb everything from natural or human life into its own imaginative body.

Another well-known poem, Wordsworth's 'I wandered lonely as a cloud', tells how Wordsworth sees a field of daffodils, and then finds later that:

They flash upon that inward eye
Which is the bliss of solitude;
And then my heart with pleasure fills,
And dances with the daffodils.

The flowers become poetic flowers as soon as they're identified with a human mind. Here we have an image from the natural world, a field of daffodils: it's enclosed inside the human mind, which puts it into the world of the imagination, and the sense of human vision and emotion radiating from the daffodils, so to speak, is what gives them their poetic magic. The human mind is Wordsworth's individual mind at first, but as soon as he writes a poem it becomes our minds too. There is no self-expression in Wordsworth's poem, because once the poem is there the individual Wordsworth has disappeared. The general principle involved is that there is really no such thing as self-expression in literature.

In other words, it isn't just the historical figure who gets taken over by literature: the poet gets taken over too. As we said in our first talk, the poet as a person is no wiser or better a man than anyone else. He's a man with a special craft of putting words together, but he may have no claim on our attention beyond that. Most of the well-known poets have well-known lives, and some of them, like Byron, have had some highly publicized love affairs. But it's only for incidental interest that we relate what a poet writes to his own life. Byron wrote a poem to a maid of Athens, and there really was a maid of Athens, a twelve-year-old girl whose price, set by her mother, was 30,000 piastres, which Byron refused to pay. Wordsworth wrote some lovely poems about a girl named Lucy, but he made Lucy up. But Lucy is just as real as the maid of Athens. With some poets, with Milton for example, we feel that here is a great man who happened to be a poet, but would still have been great whatever he did. With other equally great poets, including Homer and Shakespeare, we feel only that they were great poets. We know nothing about Homer: some people think there were two Homers or a committee of Homers. We think of a blind old man, but we get that notion from one of Homer's characters. We know nothing about Shakespeare except a signature or two, a few addresses, a will, a baptismal register, and the picture of a man who is clearly an idiot. We relate the poems and plays and novels we read and see, not to the men who wrote them, nor even directly to ourselves; we relate them to each other. Literature is a world that we try to build up and enter at the same time.

Wordsworth's poem is useful because it's one of those poems that tell you what the poet thinks he's trying to do. Here's another poem that tells you nothing, but just gives you the image—Blake's 'The Sick Rose':

O Rose, thou art sick!
The invisible worm
That flies in the night,
In the howling storm,

Has found out thy bed
Of crimson joy,
And his dark secret love
Does thy life destroy.

The author of a recent book on Blake, Hazard Adams, says he gave this poem to a class of sixty students and asked them to explain what it meant. Fifty-nine of them turned the poem into an allegory; the sixtieth was a student of horticulture who thought Blake was talking about plant disease. Now whenever you try to explain what any poem means you're bound to turn it into an allegory to some extent: there's no way out of that. Blake *isn't* talking about plant disease, but about something human, and as soon as you 'explain' his rose and worm you have to translate them into some aspect of human life and feeling. Here it's the sexual relation that seems to be closest to the poem. But the poem is not really an allegory, and so you can't feel that any explanation is adequate: its eloquence and power and magic get away from all explanations. And if it's not allegorical it's not allusive either. You can think of Eve in the Garden of Eden, standing naked among the flowers—herself a fairer flower, as Milton says—and being taught by the serpent that her nakedness, and the love that went with it, ought to be something dark and secret. This allusion, perhaps, does help you to understand the poem better, because it leads you toward the centre of Western literary imagination, and introduces you to the family of things Blake is dealing with. But the poem doesn't depend on the Bible, even though it would never have been written without the Bible. The student of horticulture got one thing right: he saw that Blake meant what he said when he talked about roses and worms, and not something else. To understand Blake's poem, then, you simply have to accept a world which is totally symbolic: a world in which roses and worms are so completely surrounded and possessed by the human mind that whatever goes on between them is identical with something going on in human life.

You remember that Theseus, in Shakespeare's *A Midsummer Night's Dream*, remarked that:

> The lunatic, the lover, and the poet
> Are of imagination all compact.

Theseus is not a literary critic; he's an amiable stuffed shirt, but just the same his remark has an important truth in it. The lunatic and the lover are trying to identify themselves with something, the lover with his mistress, the lunatic with whatever he's obsessed with. Primitive people also try to identify themselves with totems or animals or spirits. I spoke of the magic in Blake's poem: that's usually a very vague word in criticism, but magic is really a belief in identity of the same kind: the magician makes a wax image of somebody he doesn't like, sticks a pin in it, and the person it's identified with gets a pain. The poet, too, is an identifier: everything he sees in nature he identifies with human life. That's why literature, and more particularly poetry, shows the analogy to primitive minds that I mentioned in my first talk.

The difference is more important. Magic and primitive religion are forms of belief: lunacy and love are forms of experience or action. Belief and action are closely related, because what a man really believes is what his actions show that he believes. In belief you're continually concerned with questions of truth or reality: you can't believe anything unless you can say 'this is so'. But literature, we remember, never makes any statements of that kind: what the poet and novelist say is more like 'let's assume this situation'. So there can never be any religion of poetry or any set of beliefs founded on literature. When we stop believing in a religion, as the Roman world stopped believing in Jupiter and Venus, its gods become literary characters, and go back to the world of imagination. But a belief itself can only be replaced by another belief. Writers of course have their own beliefs, and it's natural to feel a special affection for the ones who seem to see things the same way we do. But we all know, or soon realize, that a writer's real greatness lies elsewhere. The world of the imagination is a world of unborn or embryonic beliefs: if you believe what you read in literature, you can, quite literally, believe anything.

So, you may ask, what is the use of studying a world of imagination where anything is possible and anything can be assumed, where there are no rights or wrongs and all arguments are equally good? One of the most obvious uses, I think, is its encouragement of tolerance. In the imagination our own beliefs are also only possibilities, but we can also see the possibilities in the beliefs of others. Bigots and fanatics seldom have any use for the arts, because they're so preoccupied with their beliefs and actions that they can't see them as also possibilities. It's possible to go to the other extreme, to be a dilettante so bemused by possibilities that one has no convictions or power to act at all. But such people are much less common than bigots, and in our world much less dangerous.

What produces the tolerance is the power of detachment in the imagination, where things are removed just out of reach of belief and action. Experience is nearly always commonplace; the present is not romantic in the way that the past is, and ideals and great visions have a way of becoming shoddy and squalid in practical life. Literature reverses this process. When experience is removed from us a bit, as the experience of the Napoleonic war is in Tolstoy's *War and Peace*, there's a tremendous increase of dignity and exhilaration. I mention Tolstoy because he'd be the last writer to try to glamorize the war itself, or pretend that its horror wasn't horrible. There is an element of illusion even in *War and Peace*, but the illusion gives us a reality that isn't in the actual experience of the war itself: the reality of proportion and perspective, of seeing what it's all about, that only detachment can give. Literature helps to give us that detachment, and so do history and philosophy and science and everything else worth studying. But literature has something more to give peculiarly its own: something as absurd and impossible as the primitive magic it so closely resembles.

The title of this talk, 'Giants in Time', comes from the last sentence of the great series of novels by Marcel Proust called *A la recherche du temps perdu*, which I'd prefer to translate quite literally as 'In Search of Lost Time'. Proust says that our ordinary experience, where everything dissolves into the past and where we never know what's coming next, can't give us any sense of reality, although we call it real life. In ordinary experience we're all in the position of a dog in a library, surrounded by a world of meaning in plain sight that we don't even know is there. Proust tells an immense long story that meanders through the life of France from the end of the nineteenth century to the beginning of the First World War, a story held together by certain recurring themes and experiences. Most of the story is a record of the jealousies and perversions and hypocrisies of 'real life', but there are occasional glimpses of an ecstasy and serenity infinitely beyond them. At the end of the series of books Proust explains (or at least his narrator explains) how one such experience takes him outside his ordinary life and also outside the time he is living it in. This is what enables him to write his book, because it makes it possible for him to look at men, not as living from moment to disappearing moment, but as 'giants immersed in time'.

The writer is neither a watcher nor a dreamer. Literature does not reflect life, but it doesn't escape or withdraw from life either: it swallows it. And the imagination won't stop until it's swallowed everything. No matter what direction we start off in, the signposts of literature always keep pointing the same way, to a world where nothing is outside the human imagination. If even time, the enemy of all living things, and to poets, at least, the most hated and feared of all tyrants, can be broken down by the imagination, anything can be. We come back to the limit of the imagination that I referred to in my first talk, a universe entirely possessed and occupied by human life, a city of which the stars are suburbs. Nobody can believe in any such universe: literature is not religion, and it doesn't address itself to belief. But if we shut the vision of it completely out of our minds, or insist on its being limited in various ways, something goes dead inside us, perhaps the one thing that it's really important to keep alive.

THE KEYS TO DREAMLAND 4

I've been trying to explain literature by putting you in a primitive situation on an uninhabited island, where you could see the imagination working in the most direct and simple way. Now let's start with our own society, and see where literature belongs in that, if it does. Suppose you're walking down the street of a Canadian city, Bloor or Granville or St. Catherine or Portage Avenue. All around you is a highly artificial society, but you don't think of it as artificial: you're so accustomed to it that you think of it as natural. But suppose your imagination plays a little trick on you of a kind that it often does play, and you suddenly feel like a complete outsider, someone who's just blown in from Mars on a flying saucer. Instantly you see how conventionalized everything is: the clothes, the shop windows, the movement of the cars in traffic, the cropped hair and shaved faces of the men, the red lips and blue eyelids that women put on because they want to conventionalize their faces, or 'look nice', as they say, which means the same thing. All this convention is pressing towards uniformity or likeness. To be outside the convention makes a person look queer, or, if he's driving a car, a menace to life and limb. The only exceptions are people who have decided to conform to different conventions, like nuns or beatniks. There's clearly a strong force making toward conformity in society, so strong that it seems to have something to do with the stability of society itself. In ordinary life even the most splendid things we can think of, like goodness and truth and beauty, all mean essentially what we're accustomed to. As I hinted just now in speaking of female make-up, most of our ideas of beauty are pure convention, and even truth has been defined as whatever doesn't disturb the pattern of what we already know.

When we move on to literature, we again find conventions, but this time we notice that they are conventions, because we're not so used to them. These conventions seem to have something to do with making literature as unlike life as possible. Chaucer represents people as making up stories in ten-syllable couplets. Shakespeare uses dramatic conventions, which means, for instance, that Iago has to smash Othello's marriage and dreams of future happiness and get him ready to murder his wife in a few minutes. Milton has two nudes in a garden haranguing each other in set speeches beginning with such lines as 'Daughter of God and Man, immortal Eve'—Eve being Adam's daughter because she's just been extracted from his ribcase. Almost every story we read demands that we accept as fact something that we know to be nonsense: that good people always win, especially in love; that murders are complicated and ingenious puzzles to be solved by logic, and so on. It isn't only popular literature that demands this: more highbrow stories are apt to be more ironic, but irony has its conventions too. If we go further back into literature, we run into such conventions as the king's rash promise, the enraged cuckold, the cruel mistress of love poetry—never anything that we or any other time would recognize as the normal behaviour of adult people, only the maddened ethics of fairyland.

Even the details of literature are equally perverse. Literature is a world where phoenixes and unicorns are quite as important as horses and dogs—and in literature some of the horses talk, like the ones in *Gulliver's Travels*. A random example is calling Shakespeare the 'swan of Avon'—he was called that by Ben Jonson. The town of Stratford, Ontario, keeps swans in its river partly as a literary allusion. Poets of Shakespeare's day hated to admit that they were writing words on a page: they always insisted that they were producing music. In pastoral poetry they might be playing a flute (or more accurately an oboe), but every other kind of poetic effort was called song, with a harp, a lyre or a lute in the background, depending on how highbrow the song was. Singing suggests birds, and so for their typical songbird and emblem of themselves, the poets chose the swan, a bird that can't sing. Because it can't sing, they made up a legend that it sang once before death, when nobody was listening. But Shakespeare didn't burst into song before his death: he wrote two plays a year until he'd made enough money to retire, and spent the last five years of his life counting his take.

So however useful literature may be in improving one's imagination or vocabulary, it would be the wildest kind of pedantry to use it directly as a guide to life. Perhaps here we see one reason why the poet is not only very seldom a person one would turn to for insight into the state of the world, but often seems even more gullible and simple-minded than the rest of us. For the poet, the particular literary conventions he adopts are likely to become, for him, facts of life. If he finds that the kind of writing he's best at has a good deal to do with fairies, like Yeats, or a white goddess, like Graves, or a life-force, like Bernard Shaw, or episcopal sermons, like T. S. Eliot, or bullfights, like Hemingway, or exasperation at social hypocrisies, as with the so-called angry school, these things are apt to take on a reality for him that seems badly out of proportion to his contemporaries. His life may imitate literature in a way that may warp or even destroy his social personality, as Byron wore himself out at thirty-four with the strain of being Byronic. Life and literature, then, are both conventionalized, and of the conventions of literature about all we can say is that they don't much resemble the conditions of life. It's when the two sets of conventions collide that we realize how different they are.

In fact, whenever literature gets too probable, too much like life, some self-defeating process, some mysterious law of diminishing returns, seems to set in. There's a vivid and expertly written novel by H. G. Wells called *Kipps*, about a lower-middle-class, inarticulate, very likeable Cockney, the kind of character we often find in Dickens. Kipps is carefully studied: he never says anything that a man like Kipps wouldn't say; he never sounds the 'h' in home or head; nothing he does is out of line with what we expect such a person to be like. It's an admirable novel, well worth reading, and yet I have a nagging feeling that there's some inner secret in bringing him completely to life that Dickens would have and that Wells doesn't have. All right, then, what would Dickens have done? Well, one of the things that Dickens often does do is write *badly*. He might have given Kipps sentimental speeches and false heroics and all sorts of inappropriate verbiage to say; and some readers would have clucked and tut-tutted over these passages and explained to each other how bad Dickens's taste was and how uncertain his hold on character could be. Perhaps they'd be right too. But we'd have had Kipps a few times the way he'd look to himself or the way he'd sometimes wish he could be: that's part of his reality, and the effect would remain with us however much we disapproved of it. Whether I'm right about this book or not, and I'm not at all sure I am, I think my general principle is right. What we'd never see except in a book is often what we go to books to find. Whatever is completely lifelike in literature is a bit of a laboratory specimen there. To bring anything really to life in literature we can't be lifelike: we have to be literature-like.

The same thing is true even of the use of language. We're often taught that prose is the language of ordinary speech, which is usually true in literature. But in ordinary life prose is no more the language of ordinary speech than one's Sunday suit is a bathing suit. The people who actually speak prose are highly cultivated and articulate people, who've read a good many books, and even they can speak prose only to each other. If you read the beautiful sentences of Elizabeth Bennett's conversation in *Pride and Prejudice*, you can see how in that book they give a powerfully convincing impression of a sensible and intelligent girl. But any girl who talked as coherently as that on a street car would be stared at as though she had green hair. It isn't only the difference between 1813 and 1962 that's involved either, as you'll see if you compare her speech with her mother's. The poet Emily Dickinson complained that everybody said 'What?' to her, until finally she practically gave up trying to talk altogether, and confined herself to writing notes.

All this is involved with the principle I've touched on before:

the difference between literary and other kinds of writing. If we're writing to convey information, or for any practical reason, our writing is an act of will and intention: we mean what we say, and the words we use represent that meaning directly. It's different in literature, not because the poet doesn't mean what he says too, but because his real effort is one of putting words together. What's important is not what he may have meant to say, but what the words themselves say when they get fitted together. With a novelist it's rather the incidents in the story he tells that get fitted together—as D. H. Lawrence says, don't trust the novelist; trust his story. That's why so much of a writer's best writing is or seems to be involuntary. It's involuntary because the forms of literature itself are taking control of it, and these forms are what are embodied in the conventions of literature. Conventions, we see, have the same role in literature that they have in life: they impose certain patterns of order and stability on the writer. Only, if they're such different conventions, it seems clear that the order of words, or the structure of literature, is different from the social order.

The absence of any clear line of connexion between literature and life comes out in the issues involved in censorship. Because of the large involuntary element in writing, works of literature can't be treated as embodiments of conscious will or intention, like people, and so no laws can be framed to control their behaviour which assume a tendency to do this or an intention of doing that. Works of literature get into legal trouble because they offend some powerful religious or political interest, and this interest in its turn usually acquires or exploits the kind of social hysteria that's always revolving around sex. But it's impossible to give legal definitions of such terms as obscenity in relation to works of literature. What happens to the book depends mainly on the intelligence of the judge. If he's a sensible man we get a sensible decision; if he's an ass we get that sort of decision, but what we don't get is a legal decision, because the basis for one doesn't exist. The best we get is a precedent tending to discourage cranks and pressure groups from attacking serious books. If you read the casebook on the trial of *Lady Chatterley's Lover*, you may remember how bewildered the critics were when they were asked what the moral effect of the book would be. They weren't putting on an act: they didn't know. Novels can only be good or bad in their own categories. There's no such thing as a morally bad novel: its moral effect depends entirely on the moral quality of its reader, and nobody can predict what that will be. And if literature isn't morally bad it isn't morally good either. I suppose one reason why *Lady Chatterley's Lover* dramatized this question so vividly was that it's a rather preachy and self-conscious book: like the Sunday-school novels of my childhood, it bores me a little because it tries so hard to do me good.

So literature has no consistent connexion with ordinary life, positive or negative. Here we touch on another important difference between structures of the imagination and structures of practical sense, which include the applied sciences. Imagination is certainly essential to science, applied or pure. Without a constructive power in the mind to make models of experience, get hunches and follow them out, play freely around with hypotheses, and so forth, no scientist could get anywhere. But all imaginative effort in practical fields has to meet the test of practicability, otherwise it's discarded. The imagination in literature has no such test to meet. You don't relate it directly to life or reality: you relate works of literature, as we've said earlier, to each other. Whatever value there is in studying literature, cultural or practical, comes from the total body of our reading, the castle of words we've built, and keep adding new wings to all the time.

So it's natural to swing to the opposite extreme and say that literature is really a refuge or escape from life, a self-contained world like the world of the dream, a world of play or make-believe to balance the world of work. Some literature is like that, and many people tell us that they only read to get away from reality for a bit. And I've suggested myself that the sense of escape, or at least detachment, does come into everybody's literary experience. But the real point of literature can hardly be that. Think of such writers as William Faulkner or François Mauriac, their great moral dignity, the intensity and compassion that they've studied the life around them with. Or think of James Joyce, spending seven years on one book and seventeen on another, and having them ridiculed or abused or banned by the customs when they did get published. Or of the poets Rilke and Valéry, waiting patiently for years in silence until what they had to say was ready to be said. There's a deadly seriousness in all this that even the most refined theories of fantasy or make-believe won't quite cover. Still, let's go along with the idea for a bit, because we're not getting on very fast with the relation of literature to life, or what we could call the horizontal perspective of literature. That seems to block us off on all sides.

The world of literature is a world where there is no reality except that of the human imagination. We see a great deal in it that reminds us vividly of the life we know. But in that very vividness there's something unreal. We can understand this more clearly with pictures, perhaps. There are trick-pictures—*trompe l'oeil,* the French call them—where the resemblance to life is very strong. An American painter of this school played a joke on his bitchy wife by painting one of her best napkins so expertly that she grabbed at the canvas trying to pull it off. But a painting as realistic as that isn't a reality but an illusion: it has the glittering unnatural clarity of a hallucination. The real realities, so to speak, are things that don't remind us directly of our own experience, but are such things as the wrath of Achilles or the jealousy of Othello, which are bigger and more intense experiences than anything we can reach—except in our imagination, which is what we're reaching with. Sometimes, as in the happy endings of comedies, or in the ideal world of romances, we seem to be looking at a pleasanter world than we ordinarily know. Sometimes, as in tragedy and satire, we seem to be looking at a world more devoted to suffering or absurdity than we ordinarily know. In literature we always seem to be looking either up or down. It's the vertical perspective that's important, not the horizontal one that looks out to life. Of course, in the greatest works of literature we get both the up and down views, often at the same time as different aspects of one event.

There are two halves to literary experience, then. Imagination gives us both a better and a worse world than the one we usually live with, and demands that we keep looking steadily at them both. I said in my first talk that the arts follow the path of the emotions, and of the tendency of the emotions to separate the world into a half that we like and a half that we don't like. Literature is not a world of dreams, but it would be if we had only one half without the other. If we had nothing but romances and comedies with happy endings, literature would express only a wish-fulfilment dream. Some people ask why poets want to write tragedies when the world's so full of them anyway, and suggest that enjoying such things has something morbid or gloating about it. It doesn't, but it might if there were nothing else in literature.

This point is worth spending another minute on. You recall that terrible scene in *King Lear* where Gloucester's eyes are put out on the stage. That's part of a play, and a play is supposed to be entertaining. Now in what sense can a scene like that be entertaining? The fact that it's not really happening is certainly important. It would be degrading to watch a real blinding scene, and far more so to get any pleasure out of watching it. Consequently, the entertainment doesn't consist in its reminding us of a real blinding scene. If it did, one of the great scenes of drama would turn into a piece of repulsive pornography. We couldn't stop anyone from reacting in this way, and it certainly wouldn't cure him, much less help the public, to start blaming or censoring Shakespeare for putting sadistic ideas in his head. But a reaction of that kind has nothing to do with drama. In a dramatic scene of cruelty and hatred we're seeing cruelty and hatred, which we know are permanently real things in human life, from the point of view of the imagination. What the imagination suggests is horror, not the paralyzing sickening horror of a real blinding scene, but an exuberant horror, full of the energy of repudiation. This is as powerful a rendering as we can ever get of life as we don't want it.

So we see that there are moral standards in literature after all, even though they have nothing to do with calling the police when we see a word in a book that's more familiar in sound than in print. One of the things Gloucester says in that scene is: 'I am tied to the stake, and I must stand the course.' In Shakespeare's day it was a favourite sport to tie a bear to a stake and set dogs on it until they killed it. The Puritans suppressed this sport, according to Macaulay, not because it gave pain to the bear but because it gave pleasure to the spectators. Macaulay may have intended his remark to be a sneer at the Puritans, but surely if the Puritans did feel this way they were one hundred per cent right. What other reason is there for abolishing public hangings? Whatever their motives, the Puritans and Shakespeare were operating in the same direction. Literature keeps presenting the most vicious things to us as entertainment, but what it appeals to is not any pleasure in these things, but the exhilaration of standing apart from them and being able to see them for what they are because they aren't really happening. The more exposed we are to this, the less likely we are to find an unthinking pleasure in cruel or evil things. As the eighteenth century said in a fine mouth-filling phrase, literature refines our sensibilities.

The top half of literature is the world expressed by such words as sublime, inspiring, and the like, where what we feel is not detachment but absorption. This is the world of heroes and gods and titans and Rabelaisian giants, a world of powers and passions and moments of ecstasy far greater than anything we meet outside the imagination. Such forces would not only absorb but annihilate us if they entered ordinary life, but luckily the protecting wall of the imagination is here too. As the German poet Rilke says, we adore them because they disdain to destroy us. We seem to have got quite a long way from our emotions with their division of things into 'I like this' and 'I don't like this'. Literature gives us an experience that stretches us vertically to the heights and depths of what the human mind can conceive, to what corresponds to the conceptions of heaven and hell in religion. In this perspective what I like or don't like disappears, because there's nothing left of me as a separate person: as a reader of literature I exist only as a representative of humanity as a whole. We'll see how important this is in the last talk.

No matter how much experience we may gather in life, we can never in life get the dimension of experience that the imagination gives us. Only the arts and sciences can do that, and of these, only literature gives us the whole sweep and range of human imagination as it sees itself. It seems to be very difficult for many people to understand the reality and intensity of literary experience. To give an example that you may think a bit irrelevant: why have so many people managed to convince themselves that Shakespeare did not write Shakespeare's plays, when there is not an atom of evidence that anybody else did? Apparently because they feel that poetry must be written out of personal experience, and that Shakespeare didn't have enough experience of the right kind. But Shakespeare's plays weren't produced by his experience: they were produced by his imagination, and the way to develop the imagination is to read a good book or two. As for us, we can't speak or think or comprehend even our own experience except within the limits of our own power over words, and those limits have been established for us by our great writers.

Literature, then, is not a dream-world: it's two dreams, a wish-fulfilment dream and an anxiety dream, that are focussed together, like a pair of glasses, and become a fully conscious vision. Art, according to Plato, is a dream for awakened minds, a work of imagination withdrawn from ordinary life, dominated by the same forces that dominate the dream, and yet giving us a perspective and dimension on reality that we don't get from any other approach to reality. So the poet and the dreamer are distinct, as Keats says. Ordinary life forms a community, and literature is among other things an art of communication, so it forms a community too. In ordinary life we fall into a private and separate subconscious every night, where we reshape the world according to a private and separate imagination. Underneath literature there's another kind of subconscious, which is social and not private, a need for forming a community around certain symbols, like the Queen and the flag, or around certain gods that represent order and stability, or becoming and change, or death and rebirth to a new life. This is the myth-making power of the human mind, which throws up and dissolves one civilization after another.

I've taken my title for this talk, 'The Keys to Dreamland', from what is possibly the greatest single effort of the literary imagination in the twentieth century, Joyce's *Finnegans Wake*. In this book a man goes to sleep and falls, not into the Freudian separate or private subconscious, but into the deeper dream of man that creates and destroys his own societies. The entire book is written in the language of this dream. It's a subconscious language, mainly English, but connected by associations and puns with the eighteen or so other languages that Joyce knew. *Finnegans Wake* is not a book to read, but a book to decipher: as Joyce says, it's about a dreamer, but it's addressed to an ideal reader suffering from an ideal insomnia. The reader or critic, then, has a role complementing the poet's role. We need two powers in literature, a power to create and a power to understand.

In all our literary experience there are two kinds of response. There is the direct experience of the work itself, while we're reading a book or seeing a play, especially for the first time. This experience is uncritical, or rather pre-critical, so it's not infallible. If our experience is limited, we can be roused to enthusiasm or carried away by something that we can later see to have been second-rate or even phoney. Then there is the conscious, critical response we make after we've finished reading or left the theatre, where we compare what we've experienced with other things of the same kind, and form a judgement of value and proportion on it. This critical response, with practice, gradually makes our pre-critical responses more sensitive and accurate, or improves our taste, as we say. But behind our responses to individual works, there's a bigger response to our literary experience as a whole, as a total possession.

The critic has always been called a judge of literature, which means, not that he's in a superior position to the poet, but that he ought to know something about literature, just as a judge's right to be on a bench depends on his knowledge of law. If he's up against something the size of Shakespeare, he's the one being judged. The critic's function is to interpret every work of literature in the light of all the literature he knows, to keep constantly struggling to understand what literature as a whole is about. Literature as a whole is not an aggregate of exhibits with red and blue ribbons attached to them, like a cat-show, but the range of articulate human imagination as it extends from the height of imaginative heaven to the depth of imaginative hell. Literature is a human apocalypse, man's revelation to man, and criticism is not a body of adjudications, but the awareness of that revelation, the last judgement of mankind.

VERTICALS OF ADAM   5

In my first four talks I've been building up a theory of literature. Now I'm ready to put this theory to a practical test. If it's any good, it should give us some guidance on the question of how to teach literature, especially to children. It should tell us what the simple and fundamental conceptions are that we should start with, and what more advanced studies can later be built on them. It seems clear that the teaching of literature needs a bit more theory of this kind, and suffers in comparison with science and mathematics from not having it.

My general principle, developed in my first four talks, is that in the history of civilization literature follows after a mythology. A myth is a simple and primitive effort of the imagination to identify the human with the non-human world, and its most typical result is a story about a god. Later on, mythology begins to merge into literature, and myth then becomes a structural principle of story-telling. I've tried to explain how myths stick together to form a mythology, and how the containing framework of the mythology takes the shape of a feeling of lost identity which we had once and may have again.

The most complete form of this myth is given in the Christian

Bible, and so the Bible forms the lowest stratum in the teaching of literature. It should be taught so early and so thoroughly that it sinks straight to the bottom of the mind, where everything that comes along later can settle on it. That, I am aware, is a highly controversial statement, and can be misunderstood in all kinds of ways, so please remember that I'm speaking as a literary critic about the teaching of literature. There are all sorts of secondary reasons for teaching the Bible as literature: the fact that it's so endlessly quoted from and alluded to, the fact that the cadences and phrases of the King James translation are built into our minds and way of thought, the fact that it's full of the greatest and best known stories we have, and so on. There are also the moral and religious reasons for its importance, which are different reasons. But in the particular context in which I'm speaking now, it's the total shape and structure of the Bible which is most important: the fact that it's a continuous narrative beginning with the creation and ending with the Last Judgement, and surveying the whole history of mankind, under the symbolic names of Adam and Israel, in between. In other words, it's the *myth* of the Bible that should be the basis of literary training, its imaginative survey of the human situation which is so broad and comprehensive that everything else finds its place inside it. Remember too that to me the word myth, like the words fable and fiction, is a technical term in criticism, and the popular sense in which it means something untrue I regard as a debasing of language. Further, the Bible may be more things than a work of literature, but it certainly is a work of literature too: no book can have had its influence on literature without itself having literary qualities. For the purpose I have in mind, however, the Bible could only be taught in school by someone with a well-developed sense of literary structure.

The first thing to be laid on top of a Biblical training, in my opinion, is Classical mythology, which gives us the same kind of imaginative framework, of a more fragmentary kind. Here again there are all sorts of incidental or secondary reasons for the study: the literatures of all modern Western languages are so full of Classical myths that one hardly knows what's going on without some training in them. But again, the primary reason is the shape of the mythology. The Classical myths give us, much more clearly than the Bible, the main episodes of the central myth of the hero whose mysterious birth, triumph and marriage, death and betrayal and eventual rebirth follow the rhythm of the sun and the seasons. Hercules and his twelve labours, Theseus emerging from his labyrinth, Perseus with the head of Medusa: these are story-themes that ought to get into the mind as early as possible. Resemblances between Biblical and Classical legend should not be treated as purely coincidental: on the contrary, it's essential to show how the same literary patterns turn up within different cultures and religions. A poet living in the days of Shakespeare or Milton got this kind of training in elementary school, and we can't read far in *Paradise Lost*, for example, without realizing not simply that we need to know both the Bible and the Classical myths to follow it, but that we also have to see the relation of the two mythologies to each other. Modern poets don't get the same kind of education, as a rule: they have to educate themselves, and some of the difficulty that people complain about in modern poets goes back to what I think is a deficiency in the earliest stages of literary teaching, for both poet and reader. I've taken the title for this talk, 'Verticals of Adam', from a series of sonnets by Dylan Thomas, 'Altarwise by owl-light', which tells the story of a 'gentleman', as Thomas calls him, who is both Adam and Apollo, and moves across the sky going through the stages of life and death and rebirth. These sonnets make very tough reading, and I think one reason why they're so obscure is that the shape of the central myth of literature broke in on Thomas suddenly at a certain stage of his development, and that it broke with such force that he could hardly get all his symbols and metaphors down fast enough. His later poems, difficult as some of them are, are still much simpler, because by that time he'd digested his mythology.

The Greeks and Romans, like the authors of the Old Testament, arranged their myths in a sequence, starting with stories of creation and fall and flood and gradually moving into historical reminiscence, and finally into actual history. And as they move into history they also move into more recognizable and fully developed forms of literature. The Classical myths produced Homer and the Greek dramatists; the ancient traditions of the Old Testament developed into the Psalms and the Book of Job.

The next step in literary teaching is to understand the structure of the great literary forms. Two of these forms are the pair familiar to us from drama, tragedy and comedy. There's also another pair of opposites, which I should call romance and irony. In romance we have a simplified and idealized world, of brave heroes, pure and beautiful heroines, and very bad villains. All forms of irony, including satire, stress the complexity of human life in opposition to this simple world. Of these four forms, comedy and romance are the primary ones; they can be taught to the youngest students. When adults read for relaxation they almost always return to either comedy or romance. Tragedy and irony are more difficult, and ought to be reserved, I think, for the secondary-school level.

Romance develops out of the story of the hero's adventures which the student has already met in myth, and comedy out of the episode of the hero's triumph or marriage. It's important to get the habit of standing back and looking at the total structure of every literary work studied. A student who acquires this habit will see how the comedy of Shakespeare he's studying has the same general structure as the battered old movie he saw on television the night before. When I was at school we had to read *Lorna Doone*, and a girl beside me used to fish a love-story magazine out of her desk and read it on her knee when the teacher wasn't looking. She obviously regarded these stories as much hotter stuff than *Lorna Doone*, and perhaps they were, but I'd be willing to bet something that they told exactly the same kind of story. To see these resemblances in structure will not, by itself, give any sense of comparative value, any notion why Shakespeare is better than the television movie. In my opinion value-judgements in literature should not be hurried. It does a student little good to be told that A is better than B, especially if he prefers B at the time. He has to feel values for himself, and should follow his individual rhythm in doing so. In the meantime, he can read almost anything in any order, just as he can eat mixtures of food that would have his elders reaching for the baking soda. A sensible teacher or librarian can soon learn how to give guidance to a youth's reading that allows for undeveloped taste and still doesn't turn him into a gourmet or a dyspeptic before his time.

It's important too that everything that has a story, such as a myth, should be read or listened to purely as a story. Many people grow up without really understanding the difference between imaginative and discursive writing. On the rare occasions when they encounter poems, or even pictures, they treat them exactly as though they were intended to be pieces of more or less disguised information. Their questions are all based on this assumption. What is he trying to get across? What am I supposed to get out of it? Why doesn't somebody explain it to me? Why couldn't he have written it in a different way so I could understand him? The art of listening to stories is a basic training for the imagination. You don't start arguing with the writer: you accept his postulates, even if he tells you that the cow jumped over the moon, and you don't react until you've taken in all of what he has to say. If Bertrand Russell is right in saying that suspension of judgement is one of the essential operations of the mind, the benefits of learning to do this go far beyond literature. And even then what you react to is the total structure of the story as a whole, not to some message or moral or Great Thought that you can snatch out of it and run away with. Equal in importance to this training is that of getting the student to write himself. No matter how little of this he does, he's bound to have the experience sooner or later of feeling he's said something that he can't explain except in exactly the same way that he's said it. That should help to make him more tolerant about difficulties he encounters in his reading, although the benefits of trying to express oneself in different literary ways naturally extend a lot further than mere tolerance.

I have to cover a good deal of ground in this talk, so I can only suggest briefly that the study of English has two contexts which must be in place for the student if his study is to have any reality. There is, first, the context of languages other than English, and there is, second, the context of the arts other than literature. The people who call themselves humanists, and who include students of literature, have always been primarily people who studied other languages. The basis of the cultural heritage of English speaking peoples is not in English; it's in Latin and Greek and Hebrew. This basis has to be given the young student in translation, although no translation of anything worth reading is of much use except as a crib to the original. Nowadays the modern languages take a more prominent place in education than the Classical ones, and it's often said that we ought to learn other languages as a kind of painful political duty. There's that, certainly, but there's also the fact that all our mental processes connected with words tend to follow the structure of the language we're thinking in. We can't use our minds at full capacity unless we have some idea of how much of what we think we're thinking is really thought, and how much is just familiar words running along their own familiar tracks. Nearly everyone does enough talking, at least, to become fairly fluent in his own language, and at that point there's always the danger of automatic fluency, turning on a tap and letting a lot of platitudinous bumble emerge. The best check on this so far discovered is some knowledge of other languages, where at least the bumble has to fit into a different set of grammatical grooves. I have a friend who was chairman of a commission that had to turn in a complicated report, where things had to be put clearly and precisely. Over and over again he'd turn to a French Canadian on the committee and ask him to say it in French, and he'd get his lead from that. This is an example of why the humanists have always insisted that you don't learn to think wholly from one language: you learn to think better from linguistic conflict, from bouncing one language off another.

And just as it's easy to confuse thinking with the habitual associations of language, so it's easy to confuse thinking with thinking in words. I've even heard it said that thought is inner speech, though how you'd apply that statement to what Beethoven was doing when he was thinking about his ninth symphony I don't know. But the study of other arts, such as painting and music, has many values for literary training apart from their value as subjects in themselves. Everything man does that's worth doing is some kind of construction, and the imagination is the constructive power of the mind set free to work on pure construction, construction for its own sake. The units don't have to be words; they can be numbers or tones or colours or bricks or pieces of marble. It's hardly possible to understand what the imagination is doing with words without seeing how it operates with some of these other units.

As the student gets older, he reads more complicated literature, and this usually means literature concerned largely or exclusively with human situations and conflicts. The old primitive association of human and natural worlds is still there in the background, but in, say, a novel of Henry James it's a long way in the background. We often feel that certain types of literature, such as fairy tales, are somehow good for the imagination: the reason is that they restore the primitive perspective that mythology has. So does modern poetry, on the whole, as compared with fiction. At this point a third context of literature begins to take shape: the relation of literature to other subjects, such as history and philosophy and the social sciences, that are built out of words.

In every properly taught subject, we start at the centre and work outwards. To try to teach literature by starting with the applied use of words, or 'effective communication', as it's often called, then gradually work into literature through the more documentary forms of prose fiction and finally into poetry, seems to me a futile procedure. If literature is to be properly taught, we have to start at its centre, which is poetry, then work outwards to literary prose, then outwards from there to the applied languages of business and professions and ordinary life. Poetry is the most direct and simple means of expressing oneself in words: the most primitive nations have poetry, but only quite well developed civilizations can produce good prose. So don't think of poetry as a perverse and unnatural way of distorting ordinary prose statements: prose is a much less natural way of speaking than poetry is. If you listen to small children, and to the amount of chanting and singsong in their speech, you'll see what I mean. Some languages, such as Chinese, have kept differences of pitch in the spoken word: where Canadians got the monotone honk that you're listening to now I don't know— probably from the Canada goose.

What poetry can give the student is, first of all, the sense of physical movement. Poetry is not irregular lines in a book, but something very close to dance and song, something to walk down street keeping time to. Even if the rhythm is free it's still something to be declaimed. The surge and sweep of Homer and the sinewy springing rhythm of Shakespeare have much the same origin: they were written that way partly because they had to be bellowed at a restless audience. Modern poets work very hard at trying to convince people in cafés or even in parks on Sunday that poetry can be performed and listened to, like a concert. There are quieter effects in poetry, of course, but a lot even of them have to do with physical movement, such as the effect of wit that we get from strict metre, from hearing words stepping along in an ordered marching rhythm. From poetry one can go on to prose, and if one's literary education is sound the first thing one should demand from prose is rhythm. My own teacher, Pelham Edgar, once told me that if the rhythm of a sentence was right, its sense could look after itself. Of course I was at university then, and I admit that this would be a dangerous thing to say to a ten-year-old. But it said one thing that was true. We're often told that to write we must have something to say, but that in its turn means having a certain potential of verbal energy.

Besides rhythm, the imagery and diction of poetry should be carried out into other modes of English. The preference of poetry for concrete and simple words, for metaphor and simile and all the figures of associative language, and its ability to contain great reserves of meaning in the simple forms that we call myths and read as stories, are equally important. The study of literature, we've been saying, revolves around certain classics or models, which the student gradually learns to read for himself. There are many reasons why certain works of literature are classics, and most of them are purely literary reasons. But there's another reason too: a great work of literature is also a place in which the whole cultural history of the nation that produced it comes into focus. I've mentioned Robinson Crusoe: you can get from that book a kind of detached vision of the British Empire, imposing its own pattern wherever it goes, catching its man Friday and trying to turn him into an eighteenth-century Nonconformist, never dreaming of 'going native', that history alone would hardly give. If you read *Anna and the King of Siam* or saw *The King and I*, you remember the story of the Victorian lady in an Oriental country which had never had any tradition of chivalry or deference to women. She expected to be treated like a Victorian lady, but she didn't so much say so as express by her whole bearing and attitude that nothing else was possible, and eventually Siam fell into line. As you read or see that story, the shadow of an even greater Victorian lady appears behind her: Alice in Wonderland, remembering the manners her governess taught her, politely starting topics of conversation and pausing for a reply, unperturbed by the fact that what she's talking to may be a mock turtle or a caterpillar, surprised only by any rudeness or similar failure to conform to the proper standards of behaviour.

This aspect of literature in which it's a kind of imaginative key to history is particularly clear in the novel, and more elusive and difficult in Shakespeare or Milton. American literature falls mainly in the period of fiction, and in such books as *Huckleberry Finn, The Scarlet Letter, Moby Dick, Walden, Uncle Tom's Cabin,* a great deal of American social life, history, religion and cultural mythology is reflected. I think it's a mistake to approach such books inside out, as is often done, starting with the history and sociology and the rest of it and treating the book as though it were an allegory of such things. The book itself is a literary form, descended from and related to other literary forms: everything else follows from that. The constructs of the imagination tell us things about human life that we don't get in any other way. That's why it's important for Canadians to pay particular attention to Canadian literature, even when the imported brands are better seasoned. I often think of a passage in Lincoln's Gettysburg address: 'The world will little note nor long remember what we say here, but it can never forget what they did here.' The Gettysburg address is a great poem, and poets have been saying ever since Homer's time that they were just following after the great deeds of the heroes, and that it was the deeds which were important and not what they said about them. So it was right, in a way, that is, it was traditional, and tradition is very important in literature, for Lincoln to say what he did. And yet it isn't really true. Nobody can remember the names and dates of battles unless they make some appeal to the imagination: that is, unless there is some literary reason for doing so. Everything that happens in time vanishes in time: it's only the imagination that, like Proust, whom I quoted earlier, can see men as 'giants in time'.

What is true of the relation of literature to history is also true of the relation of literature to thought. I said in my first talk that literature, being one of the arts, is concerned with the home and not the environment of man: it lives in a simple, man-centered world and describes the nature around it in the kind of associative language that relates it to human concerns. We notice that this man-centered perspective is in ordinary speech as well: in ordinary speech we are all bad poets. We think of things as up or down, for example, so habitually that we often forget they're just metaphors. Religious language is so full of metaphors of ascent, like 'lift up your hearts', and so full of traditional associations with the sky, that Mr. Krushchev still thinks he's made quite a point when he tells us that his astronauts can't find any trace of God in outer space. If we're being realistic instead of religious, we prefer to descend, to get 'down' to the facts (or to 'brass tacks', which is rhyming slang for the same thing). We speak of a subconscious mind which we assume is underneath the conscious mind, although so far as I know it's only a spatial metaphor that puts it there. We line up arguments facing each other like football teams: on the one hand there's this and on the other hand there's that.

All this is familiar enough, but it isn't often thought of as directly connected with one's education in literature. Still, it takes me to a point at which I can perhaps venture a suggestion about what the real place of literature in education is. I think it has somewhat the same relationship to the studies built out of words, history, philosophy, the social sciences, law, and theology, that mathematics has to the physical sciences. The pure mathematician proceeds by making postulates and assumptions and seeing what comes out of them, and what the poet or novelist does is rather similar. The great mathematical geniuses often do their best work in early life, like most of the great lyrical poets. Pure mathematics enters into and gives form to the physical sciences, and I have a notion that the myths and images of literature also enter into and give form to all the structures we build out of words.

In literature we have both a theory and a practice. The practice is the production of literature by writers of all types, from geniuses to hacks, from those who write out of the deepest agonies of the spirit to those who write for fun. The theory of literature is what I mean by criticism, the activity of uniting literature with society, and with the different contexts that literature itself has, some of which we've been looking at. The great bulk of criticism is teaching, at all levels from kindergarten to graduate school. A small part of it is reviewing, or introducing current literature to its public, and a still smaller, though of course central, part of it is scholarship and research. The importance of criticism, in this sense, has increased prodigiously in the last century or so, the reason being simply the increase in the proportion of people that education is trying to reach. If we think of any period in the past—say eighteenth-century England —we think of the writers and scholars and artists, Fielding and Johnson and Hogarth and Adam Smith and a hundred more, and the cultivated and educated audience which made their work possible. But these writers and artists and their entire public, added all together, would make up only a minute fraction of the total population of England at that time—so minute that my guess is we'd hardly believe the statistics if we had them. In these days we're in a hare-and-tortoise race between mob rule and education: to avoid collapsing into mob rule we have to try to educate a minority that'll stand out against it. The fable says the tortoise won in the end, which is consoling, but the hare shows a good deal of speed and few signs of tiring.

In my third talk I tried to distinguish the world of imagination from the world of belief and action. The first, I said, was a vision of possibilities, which expands the horizon of belief and makes it both more tolerant and more efficient. I have now tried to trace the progress of literary education to the point at which the student has acquired something of this vision and is ready to carry what he has of it into society. It's clear that the end of literary teaching is not simply the admiration of literature; it's something more like the transfer of imaginative energy from literature to the student. The student's response to this transfer of energy may be to become a writer himself, but the great majority of students will do other things with it. In my last talk I want to consider the educated imagination and what it does as it goes to work in society.

THE VOCATION OF ELOQUENCE   6

The title I'm using for this talk, 'The Vocation of Eloquence', comes from a gorgeous French poem called *Anabase*, by a writer whose pen-name is St. John Perse. It's been translated into English by T. S. Eliot. Its theme is the founding of a city and a new civilization, and naturally the author, being a poet, is keenly aware of the importance of the use of words in establishing a society. Tonight I want to move away from strict critical theory into the wider and more practical aspects of a literary training. I don't think of myself as speaking primarily to writers, or to people who want to be writers: I'm speaking to you as consumers, not producers, of literature, as people who read and form the public for literature. It's as consumers that you may want to know more about what literature can do and what its uses are, apart from the pleasure it gives.

I said at the beginning that nothing can be more obviously useful than learning to read and write and talk, but that a lot of people, especially young and inexperienced people, don't see why studying literature should be a necessary part of this. One of the things I've been trying to do in these talks is to distinguish the language of the imagination, which is literature, from two other ways of using words: ordinary speech and the conveying of information. It's probably occurred to you already that these three ways of using words overlap a good deal. Literature speaks the language of the imagination, and the study of literature is supposed to train and improve the imagination. But we use our imagination all the time: it comes into all our conversation and practical life: it even produces dreams when we're asleep. Consequently we have only the choice between a badly trained imagination and a well trained one, whether we ever read a poem or not.

When you stop to think about it, you soon realize that our imagination is what our whole social life is really based on. We have feelings, but they affect only us and those immediately around us; and feelings can't be directly conveyed by words at all. We have intelligence and a capacity for reasoning, but in ordinary life we almost never get a chance to use the intellect by itself. In practically everything we do it's the combination of emotion and intellect we call imagination that goes to work. Take, for example, the subject that in literary criticism is called rhetoric, the social or public use of words. In ordinary life, as in literature, the way you say things can be just as important as what's said. The words you use are like the clothes you wear. Situations, like bodies, are supposed to be decently covered. You may have some social job to do that involves words, such as making a speech or preaching a sermon or teaching a lesson or presenting a case to a judge or writing an obituary on a dead skinflint or reporting a murder trial or greeting visitors in a public building or writing copy for an ad. In none of these cases is it your job to tell the naked truth: we realize that even in the truth there are certain things we can say and certain things we can't say.

Society attaches an immense importance to saying the right thing at the right time. In this conception of the 'right thing', there are two factors involved, one moral and one aesthetic. They are inseparable, and equally important. Some of the right things said may be only partly true, or they may be so little of the truth as to be actually hypocritical or false, at least in the eyes of the Recording Angel. It doesn't matter: in society's eyes the virtue of saying the right thing at the right time is more important than the virtue of telling the whole truth, or sometimes even of telling the truth at all. We even have a law of libel to prevent us from telling some truths about some people unless it's in the public interest. So when Bernard Shaw remarks that a temptation to tell the truth should be just as carefully considered as a temptation to tell a lie, he's pointing to a social standard beyond the merely intellectual standards of truth and falsehood, which has the power of final veto, and which only the imagination can grasp. We find rhetorical situations everywhere in life, and only our imaginations can get us out of them. Suppose we're talking to somebody, let's say a woman, who's in a difficult mood. We're faced at once with the problem: does what she is saying represent her actual meaning, or is it just a disguised way of representing her emotional state of mind? Usually we assume the latter but pretend to be assuming the former. This is a problem in rhetoric, and our decision is an act of literary criticism. The importance of rhetoric proves, once again, that the imagination uses words to express a certain kind of social vision. The social vision of rhetoric is that of society dressed up in its Sunday clothes, people parading in front of each other, and keeping up the polite, necessary and not always true assumption that they are what they appear to be.

In our use of words in ordinary life, I said in my last talk, we are all bad poets. We read stories in our newspapers about Britain and Russia and France and India, all doing that and thinking that, as though each of these nations was an individual person. We know, of course, that such a use of language is a figure of speech, and probably a necessary figure, but sometimes we get misled by such figures. Or we get into the opposite habit of referring to the government of Canada as 'they', forgetting that they're our own employees and assuming that 'they' are carrying out plans and pursuing interests of their own. Both of these habits are forms of misapplied mythology or personification.

The central place of the imagination in social life is something that the advertisers suddenly woke up to a few years ago. Ever since, they've been doing what they call projecting the image, and hiring psychologists to tell them what makes the most direct appeal to the imagination. I spoke in my last talk of the element

THE EDUCATED IMAGINATION

of illusion in the imagination, and advertising is one example, though a very obvious one, of the deliberate creation of an illusion in the middle of real life. Our reaction to advertising is really a form of literary criticism. We don't take it literally, and we aren't supposed to: anyone who believed literally what every advertiser said would hardly be capable of managing his own affairs. I recently went past two teen-age girls looking at the display in front of a movie which told them that inside was the thrill of a lifetime, on no account to be missed, and I heard one of them say: 'Do you suppose it's any good?' That was the voice of sanity trying to get its bearings in a world of illusion. We may think of it as the voice of reason, but it's really the voice of the imagination doing its proper job. You remember that I spoke of irony, which means saying one thing and meaning another, as a device which a writer uses to detach our imaginations from a world of absurdity or frustration by letting us see around it. To protect ourselves in a society like ours, we have to look at such advertising as that movie display ironically: it means something to us which is different from what it says. The end of the process is not to reject all advertising, but to develop our own vision of society to the point at which we can choose what we want out of what's offered to us and let the rest go. What we choose is what fits that vision of society.

This principle holds not only for advertising but for most aspects of social life. During an election campaign, politicians project various images on us and make speeches which we know to be at best a carefully selected part of the truth. We tend to look down on the person who responds to such appeals emotionally: we feel he's behaving childishly and like an irresponsible citizen if he allows himself to be stampeded. Of course there's often a great sense of release in a purely emotional response. Hitler represented to Germany a tremendous release from its frustrations and grievances by simply acting like a three-year-old child: when he wanted something he went into a tantrum and screamed and chewed the scenery until he got it. But that example shows how dangerous the emotional response is, and how right we are to distrust it. So we say we ought to use our reason instead. But all the appeals to us are carefully rationalized, except the obviously crackpot ones, and we still have to make a choice.

What the responsible citizen really uses is his imagination, not believing anybody literally, but voting for the man or party that corresponds most closely, or least remotely, to his vision of the society he wants to live in. The fundamental job of the imagination in ordinary life, then, is to produce, out of the society we have to live in, a vision of the society we want to live in. Obviously that can't be a separated society, so we have to understand how to relate the two.

The society we have to live in, which for us happens to be a twentieth-century Canadian society, presents our imagination with its own substitute for literature. This is a social mythology, with its own folklore and its own literary conventions, or what corresponds to them. The purpose of this mythology is to persuade us to accept our society's standards and values, to 'adjust' to it, as we say. Every society produces such a mythology: it's a necessary part of its coherence, and we have to accept some of it if we're to live in it, even things that we don't believe. The more slowly a society changes, the more solidly based its mythology seems to be. In the Middle Ages the mythology of protection and obedience seemed one of the eternal verities, something that could never change. But change it did, at least all of it that depended on a certain kind of social structure. A hundred years ago a mythology of independence, hard work, thrift and saving for a rainy day looked equally immortal, but, again, everything that was based on weak social services and stable values of money had to go. If a society changes very rapidly, and our society certainly does, we have to recognize the large element of illusion in all social mythology as a simple matter of self-protection. The first thing our imaginations have to do for us, as soon as we can handle words well enough to read and write and talk, is to fight to protect us from falling into the illusions that society threatens us with. The illusion is itself produced by the social imagination, of course, but it's an inverted form of imagination. What it creates is the imaginary, which as I said earlier is different from the imaginative.

The main elements of this social mythology will be familiar to you as soon as I mention them. I spoke of advertising, and what's illusory about that is the perverted appeal it so often makes to the imagination: the appeals to snobbery and to what are called 'status symbols', the exploiting of the fear of being ridiculed or isolated from society, the suggestion of an easy way of getting on the inside track of what's going on, and so on. Then there's the use of cliché, that is, the use of ready-made, prefabricated formulas designed to give those who are too lazy to think the illusion of thinking. The Communists of course have made a heavy industry of clichés, but we have our own too. Hard-headed business man; ivory tower; longhair; regimentation; togetherness; airy-fairy. Anybody who believes literally what these clichés express, as far as any thinking for himself is concerned, might just as well be in Moscow reading about fascist hyenas and the minions of imperialist aggression.

Then there's the use of what we call jargon or gobbledegook, or what people who live in Washington or Ottawa call federal prose, the gabble of abstractions and vague words which avoids any simple or direct statement. There's a particular reason for using gobbledegook which makes it a part of social mythology. People write this way when they want to sound as impersonal as possible, and the reason why they want to sound impersonal is that they want to suggest that the social machine they're operating, usually a government agency, is running smoothly, and that no human factors are going to disturb it. Direct and simple language always has some force behind it, and the writers of gobbledegook don't want to be forceful; they want to be soothing and reassuring. I remember a report on the classification of government documents which informed me that some documents were eventually classified for permanent deposition. The writer meant that he threw them away. But he didn't want to say so, and suggest that somebody was actually tearing up paper and aiming it at a waste-basket; he wanted to suggest some kind of invisible perfect processing. We get similar euphemisms in military writing, where we read about 'anti-personnel bombs', meaning bombs that kill men, designed not to give us any uncomfortable images of legs torn off and skulls blown open. We can see here how the ordinary use of rhetoric, which attempts to make society presentable, is becoming hypocritical and disguising the reality it presents beyond the level of social safety.

Then there's all the mythology about the 'good old days', when everything was simpler and more leisurely and everybody was much closer to nature and got their milk out of cows instead of out of bottles. Literary critics call these reveries pastoral myths, because they correspond to the same kind of convention in literature that produces stories about happy shepherds and milkmaids. Many people like to assume that the society of their childhood was a solid and coherent structure which is now falling apart, as morals have become looser and social conditions more chaotic and the arts more unintelligible to ordinary people, and so forth. Some time ago an archaeologist in the Near East dug up an inscription five thousand years old which told him that 'children no longer obey their parents, and the end of the world is rapidly approaching'. It's characteristic of such social myth-making that it can swing from one extreme to the other without any sense of inconsistency, and so we also have progress myths, of the kind that rationalize the spreading of filling stations and suburban bungalows and four-lane highways over the Canadian landscape. Progress myths come into all the phoney history that people use when they say that someone is a 'Puritan', meaning that he's a prude, or that someone else is 'medieval' or 'mid-Victorian', meaning that he's old-fashioned. The effect of such words is to give the impression that all past history was a kind of bad dream, which in these enlightened days we've shaken off.

I mentioned in my last talk the various diagrams and doodles that people carry around in their minds to help them sort things out. Sometimes they sort things the wrong way. For instance, there's the diagram of left-wing and right-wing in politics, where you start with Communism at the extreme left and go around to Fascism at the extreme right. We use this diagram all the time, but suppose I were to say: 'the Conservatives are nearer to being Fascists than the Liberals, and the Liberals are nearer to being Communists than the Conservatives.' You recognize that statement to be nonsense; but if it's nonsense, the diagram it's founded on is more misleading than it is useful. The person it's most useful to is the person who wants to turn abusive, which is my next point.

Ordinary speech is largely concerned with registering our reactions to what goes on outside us. In all such reactions there's a large automatic or mechanical element. And if our only aim is to say what gets by in society, our reactions will become almost completely mechanical. That's the direction in which the use of clichés takes us. In a society which changes rapidly, many things happen that frighten us or make us feel threatened. People who can do nothing but accept their social mythology can only try to huddle more closely together when they feel frightened or threatened, and in that situation their clichés turn hysterical. Naturally that doesn't make them any less mechanical. Some years ago, in a town in the States, I heard somebody say 'those yellow bastards', meaning the Japanese. More recently, in another town, I heard somebody else use the same phrase, but meaning the Chinese. There are many reasons, not connected with literary criticism, why nobody should use a phrase like that about anybody. But the literary reason is that the phrase is pure reflex: it's no more a product of a conscious mind than the bark of a dog is.

We said that the person who is surrounded with advertisers, or with politicians at election time, neither believes everything literally nor rejects everything, but chooses in accordance with his own vision of society. The essential thing is the power of choice. In wartime this power of choice is greatly curtailed, and we resign ourselves to living by half-truths for the duration. In a totalitarian state the competition in propaganda largely disappears, and consequently the power of imaginative choice is sealed off. In our hatred and fear of war and of totalitarian government, one central element is a sense of claustrophobia that the imagination develops when it isn't allowed to function properly. This is the aspect of tyranny that's so prominently displayed in George Orwell's *1984*. Orwell even goes so far as to suggest that the only way to make tyranny permanent and unshakable, the only way in other words to create a literal hell on earth, is deliberately to debase our language by turning our speech into an automatic gabble. The fear of being reduced to such a life is a genuine fear, but of course as soon as we express it in hysterical clichés we are in the same state ourselves. As the poet William Blake says in describing something very similar, we become what we behold.

Too often the study of literature, or even the study of language, is thought of as a kind of elegant accomplishment, a matter of talking good grammar or keeping up with one's reading. I'm trying to show that the subject is a little more serious than that. I don't see how the study of language and literature can be separated from the question of free speech, which we all know is fundamental to our society. The area of ordinary speech, as I see it, is a battleground between two forms of social speech, the speech of a mob and the speech of a free society. One stands for cliché, ready-made idea and automatic babble, and it leads us inevitably from illusion into hysteria. There can be no free speech in a mob: free speech is one thing a mob can't stand. You notice that the people who allow their fear of Communism to become hysterical eventually get to screaming that every sane man they see is a Communist. Free speech, again, has nothing to do with grousing or saying that the country's in a mess and that all politicians are liars and cheats, and so on and so on. Grousing never gets any further than clichés of this kind, and the sort of vague cynicism they express is the attitude of somebody who's looking for a mob to join.

You see, freedom has nothing to do with lack of training; it can only be the product of training. You're not free to move unless you've learned to walk, and not free to play the piano unless you practice. Nobody is capable of free speech unless he knows how to use language, and such knowledge is not a gift: it has to be learned and worked at. The only exceptions, and they are exceptions that prove the rule, are people who, in some crisis, show that they have a social imagination strong and mature enough to stand out against a mob. In the recent row over desegregation in New Orleans, there was one mother who gave her reasons for sending her children to an integrated school with such dignity and precision that the reporters couldn't understand how a woman who never got past grade six learned to talk like the Declaration of Independence. Such people already have what literature tries to give. For most of us, free speech is cultivated speech, but cultivating speech is not just a skill, like playing chess. You can't cultivate speech, beyond a certain point, unless you have something to say, and the basis of what you have to say is your vision of society. So while free speech may be, at least at present, important only to a very small minority, that very small minority is what makes the difference between living in Canada and living in East Berlin or South Africa. The next question is:

where do the standards of a free society come from? They don't come from that society itself, as we've just seen.

Let us suppose that some intelligent man has been chasing status symbols all his life, until suddenly the bottom falls out of his world and he sees no reason for going on. He can't make his solid gold cadillac represent his success or his reputation or his sexual potency any more: now it seems to him only absurd and a little pathetic. No psychiatrist or clergyman can do him any good, because his state of mind is neither sick nor sinful: he's wrestling with his angel. He discovers immediately that he wants more education, and he wants it in the same way that a starving man wants food. But he wants education of a particular kind. His intelligence and emotions may quite well be in fine shape. It's his imagination that's been starved and fed on shadows, and it's education in that that he specifically wants and needs.

What has happened is that he's so far recognized only one society, the society he has to live in, the middle-class twentieth-century Canadian society that he sees around him. That is, the society he does live in is identical with the one he wants to live in. So all he has to do is to adjust to that society, to see how it works and find opportunities for getting ahead in it. Nothing wrong with that: it's what we all do. But it's not all of what we all do. He's beginning to realize that if he recognizes no other society except the one around him, he can never be anything more than a parasite on that society. And no mentally healthy man wants to be a parasite: he wants to feel he has some function, something to contribute to the world, something that would make the world poorer if he weren't in it. But as soon as that notion dawns in the mind, the world we live in and the world we want to live in become different worlds. One is around us, the other is a vision inside our minds, born and fostered by the imagination, yet real enough for us to try to make the world we see conform to its shape. This second world is the world we want to live in, but the word 'want' is now appealing to something impersonal and unselfish in us. Nobody can enter a profession unless he makes at least a gesture recognizing the ideal existence of a world beyond his own interests: a world of health for the doctor, of justice for the lawyer, of peace for the social worker, a redeemed world for the clergyman, and so on.

I'm not wandering away from my subject, or at least I'm trying not to. My subject is the educated imagination, and education is something that affects the whole person, not bits and pieces of him. It doesn't just train the mind: it's a social and moral development too. But now that we've discovered that the imaginative world and the world around us are different worlds, and that the imaginative world is more important, we have to take one more step. The society around us looks like the real world, but we've just seen that there's a great deal of illusion in it, the kind of illusion that propaganda and slanted news and prejudice and a great deal of advertising appeal to. For one thing, as we've been saying, it changes very rapidly, and people who don't know of any other world can never understand what makes it change. If Canada in 1962 is a different society from the Canada of 1942, it can't be real society, but only a temporary appearance of real society. And just as it looks real, so this ideal world that our imaginations develop inside us looks like a dream that came out of nowhere, and has no reality except what we put into it. But it isn't. It's the real world, the real form of human society hidden behind the one we see. It's the world of what humanity has done, and therefore can do, the world revealed to us in the arts and sciences. This is the world that won't go away, the world out of which we built the Canada of 1942, are now building the Canada of 1962, and will be building the quite different Canada of 1982.

A hundred years ago the Victorian poet and critic Matthew Arnold pointed out that we live in two environments, an actual social one and an ideal one, and that the ideal one can only come from something suggested in our education. Arnold called this ideal environment culture, and defined culture as the best that has been thought and said. The word culture has different overtones to most of us, but Arnold's conception is a very important one, and I need it at this point. We live, then, in both a social and a cultural environment, and only the cultural environment, the world we study in the arts and sciences, can provide the kind of standards and values we need if we're to do anything better than adjust.

I spoke in my first talk of three levels of the mind, which we have now seen to be also three forms of society and three ways of using words. The first is the level of ordinary experience and of self-expression. On this level we use words to say the right thing at the right time, to keep the social machinery running, faces saved, self-respect preserved, and social situations intact. It's not the noblest thing that words can do, but it's essential, and it creates and diffuses a social mythology, which is a structure of words developed by the imagination. For we find that to use words properly even in this way we have to use our imaginations, otherwise they become mechanical clichés, and get further and further removed from any kind of reality. There's something in all of us that wants to drift toward a mob, where we can all say the same thing without having to think about it, because everybody is all alike except people that we can hate or persecute. Every time we use words, we're either fighting against this tendency or giving in to it. When we fight against it, we're taking the side of genuine and permanent human civilization.

This is the world revealed by philosophy and history and science and religion and law, all of which represent a more highly organized way of using words. We find knowledge and information in these studies, but they're also structures, things made out of words by a power in the human mind that constructs and builds. This power is the imagination, and these studies are its products. When we think of their content, they're bodies of knowledge; when we think of their form, they're myths, that is, imaginative verbal structures. So the whole subject of the use of words revolves around this constructive power itself, as it operates in the art of words, which is literature, the laboratory where myths themselves are studied and experimented with.

The particular myth that's been organizing this talk, and in a way the whole series, is the story of the Tower of Babel in the Bible. The civilization we live in at present is a gigantic technological structure, a skyscraper almost high enough to reach the moon. It looks like a single world-wide effort, but it's really a deadlock of rivalries; it looks very impressive, except that it has no genuine human dignity. For all its wonderful machinery, we know it's really a crazy ramshackle building, and at any time may crash around our ears. What the myth tells us is that the Tower of Babel is a work of human imagination, that its main elements are words, and that what will make it collapse is a confusion of tongues. All had originally one language, the myth says. That language is not English or Russian or Chinese or any common ancestor, if there was one. It is the language of human nature, the language that makes both Shakespeare and Pushkin authentic poets, that gives a social vision to both Lincoln and Gandhi. It never speaks unless we take the time to listen in leisure, and it speaks only in a voice too quiet for panic to hear. And then all it has to tell us, when we look over the edge of our leaning tower, is that we are not getting any nearer heaven, and that it is time to return to the earth.